SURVIVAL KOREAN

for Travelers and Expats
Phrases and tips to make your stay in Korea easy

SURVIVAL KOREAN

for Travelers and Expats
Phrases and tips to make your stay in Korea easy

Written by
TalkToMeInKorean
& Keith Kim

CONTENTS

HOW TO USE THIS BOOK

Being able to communicate in the local language will bring your travel experience to another level. Whether you are just passing through or living abroad, knowing a little bit can go a long way.

For decades, South Korea was a very homogenous and monolingual country. Recently, however, Korean society has become more international and there are an increasing number of Korean people who speak English. Not everyone speaks English, or feels comfortable enough to speak English with someone, so there may be situations where, if you don't know any Korean at all, you will struggle to communicate.

With this book, we make communication less of a struggle and more of a survival tool. We introduce the most essential Korean phrases and provide culture tips to help you better understand certain aspects of Korean culture. You don't have to sit down and memorize every single page from cover to cover; just open up this book whenever you want or need and flip to the section that pertains to whatever situation you are in. You can even carry this book around with you while in Korea and just show a phrase in the book to a local person if you don't feel comfortable enough to speak. However you decide to use this book, we hope you find it helpful and enjoyable!

INTRODUCTION TO 한글 (HAN-GEUL)

The Korean alphabet is called 한글 (Han-geul), and there are 24 basic letters and digraphs in 한글.

*digraph: pair of characters used to make one sound (phoneme)

Of the letters, 14 are consonants (자음) and five of them are doubled to form the five tense consonants (쌍자음).

Consonants

Basic	ㄱ	ㄴ	ㄷ	ㄹ	ㅁ	ㅂ	ㅅ	ㅇ	ㅈ	ㅊ	ㅋ	ㅌ	ㅍ	ㅎ
	g/k	n	d/t	r/l	m	b/p	s	ng	j	ch	k	t	p	h
	g/k	n	d/t	r/l	m	b/p	s/ɕ	ŋ	dʑ/tɕ	tɕh	k/kh	t/th	p/ph	h
Tense	ㄲ		ㄸ			ㅃ	ㅆ		ㅉ					
	kk		tt			pp	ss		jj					
	k'		t'			p'	s'		c'					

When it comes to vowels (모음), there are 10 basic letters. 11 additional letters can be created by combining certain basic letters to make a total of 21 vowels. Of the vowels, eight are single pure vowels, also known as monophthongs (단모음), and 13 are diphthongs (이중모음), or two vowel sounds joined into one syllable which creates one sound.

* When saying a monophthong, you are producing one pure vowel with no tongue movement.

* When saying a diphthong, you are producing one sound by saying two vowels. Therefore, your tongue and mouth move quickly from one letter to another (glide or slide) to create a single sound.

Vowels

Monophthongs

ㅏ	ㅓ	ㅗ	ㅜ	ㅡ	ㅣ	ㅐ	ㅔ
a	eo	o	u	eu	i	ae	e
a/aː	ʌ/əː	o/oː	u/uː	i/ɯː	i/iː	ɛ/ɛː	e/eː

Diphthongs

ㅑ	ㅕ	ㅛ	ㅠ		ㅒ	ㅖ
ya	yeo	yo	yu		yae	ye
ja	jʌ	jo	ju		jɛ	je

ㅘ	ㅝ				ㅙ	ㅞ
wa	wo				wae	we
wa	wʌ/wəː				wɛ	we

					ㅚ	ㅟ	ㅢ
					oe	wi	ui
					we	wi	ïi

* ㅚ and ㅟ were pronounced as single pure vowels (monophthongs) in the past; however, presently, these vowels are produced as two vowels gradually gliding into one another to create one sound (diphthong).

WRITING 한글 LETTERS

한글 is written top to bottom, left to right. For example:

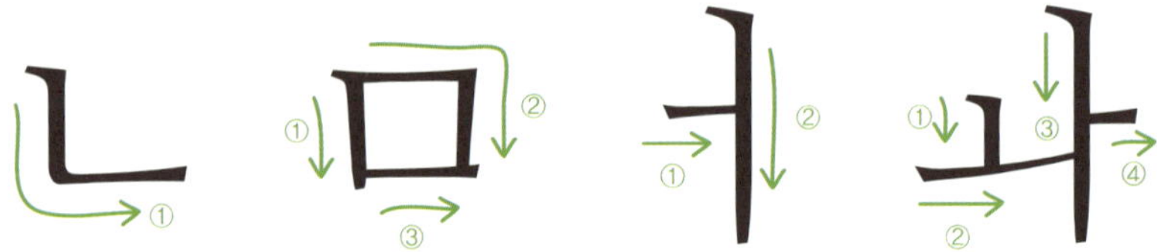

By making sure you follow the stroke order rules, you will find that writing Korean is quite easy and other people will be able to better read your handwriting.

SYLLABLE BLOCKS

Each Korean syllable is written in a way that forms a block–like shape, with each letter inside the block forming a sound/syllable.

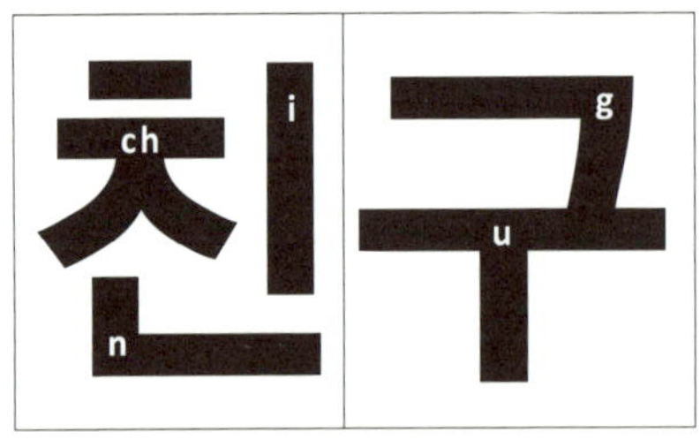

In each syllable block, there is a:

1. * Beginning consonant
2. * Middle vowel
3. Optional final consonant

* Required in a syllable block. A block MUST contain a minimum of two letters: 1 consonant and 1 vowel.

ㅊ + ㅣ + ㄴ (ch+i+n) = chin

ㄱ + ㅜ (g+u) = gu

친 (chin) + 구 (gu) = 친구 (chingu) = "friend"

Two of the most common ways to write consonant and vowel combinations in Korean are horizontally and vertically (the boxes drawn here are for illustrative purpose only).

By adding a final consonant (받침), the blocks are modified:

There are also syllables which have two final consonants, such as:

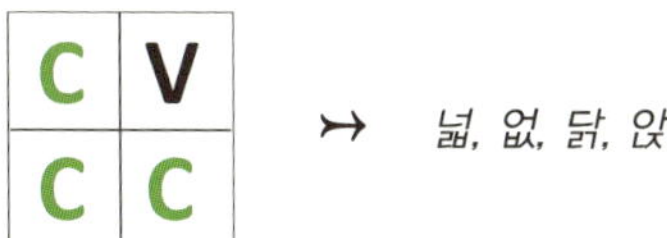

*In all the syllable blocks, the letters are either compressed or stretched to keep the size relatively the same as the other letters.

Since the "minimum two letter" rule exists and one letter has to be a consonant and the other has to be a vowel, what can you do when a vowel needs to be written in its own syllable block? Add the consonant ㅇ[ng] in front of or on top of the vowel. When reading a vowel, such as 아, the ㅇ makes no sound and you just pronounce the ㅏ [a].

*Vowels absolutely, cannot, under any circumstances be written by themselves!!

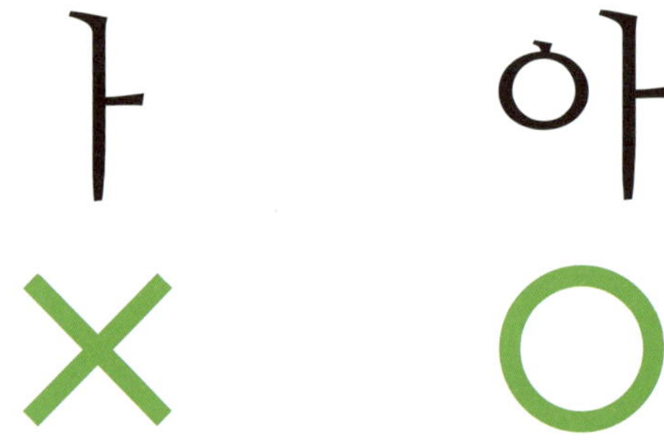

OKAY! NOW THAT YOU ARE EQUIPPED WITH A VERY BASIC KNOWLEDGE OF 한글, YOU'LL BE ABLE TO BETTER UNDERSTAND KOREAN SENTENCE STRUCTURE!

HOW SENTENCES ARE STRUCTURED IN KOREAN

Korean sentence structure is different from English. The basic English sentence structure is Subject – Verb – Object (SVO), where as in Korean is Subject – Object – Verb (SOV). For example:

English: I (subject) love (verb) you (object). = I love you.
Korean: 저는 [jeo-neun] (subject) 당신을 [dang-si-neul] (object) 사랑합니다. [sa-rang-ham-ni-da.] (verb) (literal translation) I you love. = I love you.

In Korean, if it is clear within the context of the sentence, the subject and/or object are often omitted. For example:

사랑합니다. [sa-rang-ham-ni-da.] (verb) = I love you.

HOW PARTICLES WORK IN KOREAN

Particles in Korean are words that mark the role of a noun or pronoun and can ONLY be used with nouns or pronouns. There are many different types of particles in Korean that have specific roles, including marking the object of a verb, marking the subject of a sentence, marking location, marking time, just to name a few. You will see some of these particles used in the expressions introduced in this book. For a beginner learner, the concept of particles might seem difficult, but using particles will actually come in handy since you will be able to identify the role of a noun even without hearing or looking at the entire sentence.

HOW TO USE NUMBERS IN KOREAN

Like in many other parts of the world, Korea uses the Arabic numeral system, making it quite easy to recognize numbers on a menu, signs, or the side of a bus in Korea. However, when reading numbers in Korean, there are two different number systems: native Korean numbers and sino-Korean numbers. People will generally understand you if you use one or the other set of numbers for every situation, but each set has specific situations or contexts in which they will sound most natural.

SINO-KOREAN NUMBERS

Sino-Korean numbers are based on the Chinese language. In the past, China influenced many things in Korea, even the Korean language. Many Korean words have Chinese language roots and are sometimes represented by Chinese characters (called 한자 [han-jja] in Korean). The sino-Korean number system is as follows:

일 [il]	1	십 [sip]	10
이 [i]	2	십일 [si-bil]	11
삼 [sam]	3	이십 [i-sip]	20
사 [sa]	4	삼십이 [sam-si-bi]	32
오 [o]	5	백 [baek]	100
육 [yuk]	6	천 [cheon]	1,000
칠 [chil]	7	만 [man]	10,000
팔 [pal]	8	십만 [sim-man]	100,000
구 [gu]	9	백만 [baeng-man]	1,000,000

NATIVE KOREAN NUMBERS

Some native Korean numbers have to be conjugated to an adjective form to be used with various counters. People will understand if you use the dictionary form for these numbers, but it's much more natural to use the adjective forms when used with counters. In the list below, adjective forms are in parenthesis when different from the dictionary form.

하나 [ha-na]	1 (한 [han])	열하나 [yeol-ha-na]	11
둘 [dul]	2 (두 [du])	스물 [seu-mul]	20 (스무 [seu-mu])
셋 [set]	3 (세 [se])	스물둘 [seu-mul-dul]	22 (스물두 [seu-mul-du])
넷 [net]	4 (네 [ne])	서른 [seo-reun]	30
다섯 [da-seot]	5	마흔 [ma-heun]	40
여섯 [yeo-seot]	6	쉰 [swin]	50
일곱 [il-gop]	7	예순 [ye-sun]	60
여덟 [yeo-deol]	8	일흔 [il-heun]	70
아홉 [a-hop]	9	여든 [yeo-deun]	80
열 [yeol]	10	아흔 [a-heun]	90

Things are about to get interesting!

From number 1 through 99, the usage of native Korean numbers is very distinct from the usage of sino-Korean numbers, but only for bigger units like 100, 1,000, 10,000, etc. The words for these bigger numbers in native Korean numbers are no longer used and only sino-Korean numbers are used.

Therefore, 100 in sino-Korean number is 백 [baek], and even when you think you need to use the native Korean number for something over 99, use sino-Korean.

101 = 백 [baek] (Sino-Korean) + 하나 [ha-na] (native Korean)
205 = 이 [i] (Sino-Korean) + 백 [baek] (Sino-Korean) + 다섯 [da-seot] (native Korean)

WHICH NUMBER SYSTEM DO I USE?

The counter you need to use will determine which number system to use.
Use **SINO-KOREAN NUMBERS** when you talk about...

1. Food servings (- 인분 [in-bun])
일 인분 [i rin-bun], 이 인분 [i in-bun], 삼 인분 [sa min-bun], 사 인분 [sa in-bun], 오 인분 [o in-bun]

2. Money (- 원 [won])
천 원 [cheon won], 천오백 원 [cheo-no-baek won], 오천 원 [o-cheo nwon], 만 원 [ma nwon], 삼만 원 [sam-ma nwon], 오만 이천칠백 원 [o-man i-cheon-chil-bae gwon], 십만 원 [sim-ma nwon], 백만 원 [baeng-ma nwon]

3. The date (yy, mm, dd) (- 년 [nyeon] – 월 [wol] – 일 [il])
이천십삼 년 [i-cheon-sip-ssam nyeon], 이천십사 년 [i-cheon-sip-ssa nyeon]
일 월 [i rwol], 이 월 [i wol], 삼 월 [sa mwol], 사 월 [sa wol], 오 월 [o wol], 유 월* [yu wol], 칠 월 [chi rwol], 팔 월 [pa rwol], 구 월 [gu wol], 시 월* [si wol], 십일 월 [si-bi rwol], 십이 월 [si-bi wol]
일 일 [i ril], 이 일 [i il], 십 일 [si bil], 십오 일 [si-bo il], 이십 일 [i-si bil], 삼십일 일 [sam-si-bi ril]

*When talking about months, for June and October, 육 [yuk] becomes 유 [yu] and 십 [sip] becomes 시 [si] in front of - 월 [wol].

Use **NATIVE KOREAN NUMBERS** when you talk about...

1. Inanimate items in general (-개 [gae])
한 개 [han gae], 두 개 [du gae], 세 개 [se gae], 네 개 [ne gae], 다섯 개 [da-seot kkae], 열 개 [yeol kkae], 스무 개 [seu-mu gae], 스물한 개 [seu-mul-han gae], 서른 개 [seo-reun gae], 백 개 [baek kkae], 백다섯 개 [baek-da-seot kkae]

2. Person (– 명 [myeong]: casual / – 분 [bun]: honorific)

한 명 [han myeong], 열 명 [yeol myeong], 스무 명 [seu-mu myeong], 백 명 [baeng myeong], 이백여섯 명 [i-baeng-yeo-seon myeong]

두 분 [du bun], 네 분 [ne bun], 이백 분 [i-baek ppun]

3. Age (– 살 [sal])

한 살 [han sal], 두 살 [du sal], 스무 살 [seu-mu sal], 스물세 살 [seu-mul-se sal], 스물일곱 살 [seu-mu-ril-gop ssal], 서른다섯 살[seo-reun-da-seot ssal], 마흔두 살 [ma-heun-du sal], 쉰한 살 [swin-han sal], 예순여덟 살 [ye-sun-yeo-deol ssal]

*You can use Sino-Korean numbers with the counter – 세 [se] to tell your age in more formal situations. In everyday conversations, (native Korean number) + – 살 is more commonly used.

4. bowl of rice/soup/noodle/etc. (– 그릇 [geu-reut])

한 그릇 [han geu-reut], 두 그릇 [du geu-reut], 세 그릇 [se geu-reut], 열 그릇 [yeol geu-reut/yeol kkeu-reut]

5. plates of side dishes (– 접시 [jeop-ssi])

세 접시 [se jeop-ssi], 열 접시 [yeol jjeop-ssi], 열다섯 접시 [yeol-da-seot jjeop-ssi]

*Normally, 그릇 is a counter for a bowl/serving of rice, soup, or noodle, and 접시 is for plate/serving of side dishes. Regardless of the food, if the food is served in a bowl, people use 그릇, and if the food is served on a plate, people use 접시.

6. cup / glass (– 잔 [jan])

한 잔 [han jan], 두 잔 [du jan], 세 잔 [se jan], 네 잔 [ne jan], 다섯 잔 [da-seot jjan], 여섯 잔 [yeo-seot jjan], 열한 잔 [yeol-han jan], 스물두 잔 [seu-mul-du jan]

7. bottle (– 병 [byeong])

다섯 병 [da-seot ppyeong], 열 병 [yeol byeong/yeol ppyeong] , 스물여섯 병 [seu-mul-yeo-seot ppyeong]

8. clothes (– 벌 [beol])

두 벌 [du beol], 일곱 벌 [il-gop ppeol], 열여덟 벌 [yeol-yeo-deol ppeol]

9. paper/ticket (– 장 [jang])

한 장 [han jang], 마흔일곱 장 [ma-heun-il-gop jjang], 삼백두 장 [sam-baek-du jang]

10. book (– 권 [gwon])

쉰다섯 권 [swin-da-seot kkwon], 여든일곱 권 [yeo-deun-il-gop kkwon], 아흔세 권 [a-heun-se gwon]

For the hour (- 시 [si]), you need a native Korean number. For the minute (- 분 [bun]) and the second (- 초 [cho]), you need to use Sino-Korean numbers.

한 시 이십 분 [han si i-sip ppun] (1:20), 두 시 삼십 분 [du si sam-sip ppun] (2:30), 열두 시 [yeol-du si] (12:00), 세 시 십오 분 이십일 초 [se si si-bo bun i-si-bil cho] (3:15:21)

HOW TO ASK FOR WHAT YOU WANT WITHOUT KNOWING THE NAME OF IT IN KOREAN

Knowing demonstratives (this, that, over there, etc.) can come in handy, especially if you don't know the names of the things you want. If you don't know the name of a food you want to try, a clothing item, or the name of a place on your map, point to the item/direction/place and use these simple Korean words:

this = this thing = 이거 [i-geo]
that = that thing = 저거 [jeo-geo] / 그거 [geu-geo]
*If the item is close to the person you are talking to, use 그거 [geu-geo], and if it's far from both of you, use 저거 [jeo-geo].
there = 저기 [jeo-gi]
over there = 저쪽 [jeo-jjok]
here = 여기 [yeo-gi]
over here = 이쪽 [i-jjok]

Sample Sentences

이거 주세요. [i-geo ju-se-yo.] = Please give me this one.
저거 얼마예요? [jeo-geo eol-ma-ye-yo?] = How much is that?
저쪽으로 가세요. [jeo-jjo-geu-ro ga-se-yo.] = Go that way.
여기 어떻게 가요? [yeo-gi eo-tteo-ke ga-yo?] = How can I get here?

HOW TO AGREE OR DISAGREE IN KOREAN

While most Korean people will most likely to understand if you say "yes" or "no", learning how to say these terms in Korean will pleasantly surprise the people who you are talking with.

Yes. = 네. [ne.]
No. = 아니요. [a-ni-yo.]
That's correct. = That's right. = 맞아요. [ma-ja-yo.]
It's okay. = It's fine. = 괜찮아요. [gwaen-cha-na-yo.]

HOW TO ASK A QUESTION IN KOREAN

With these interrogatives (when, why, where, etc.), you can ask questions in Korean easily:

why = 왜 [wae]
when = 언제 [eon-je]
where = 어디 [eo-di]
who = 누구 [nu-gu]
what = 무엇 [mu-eot]
which = 어느 것 [eo-neu geot]
how = 어떻게 [eo-tteo-ke]

In English, people sometimes add prepositions to specify a question, but it is important to note that by adding different particles in Korean, you can specify your question or you can use it as a subject or an object. The following are examples of the interrogative + particle structure:

until when = **언제까지** [eon-je-kka-ji]

where to = **어디로** [eo-di-ro]

where/in what place = **어디에서** [eo-di-e-seo]

who (subject) = **누가** [nu-ga]

whom = **누구를** [nu-gu-reul]

what (subject) = **무엇이** [mu-eo-si] (**무엇이** is often shortened to **뭐가** [mwo-ga] in spoken language)

what (object) = **무엇을** [mu-eo-seul] (**무엇을** is often shortened to **뭐를** [mwo-reul] in spoken language)

ESSENTIAL WORDS AND PHRASES

안녕하세요. [an-nyeong-ha-se-yo.] = Hello.

안녕히 계세요. [an-nyeong-hi gye-se-yo.] = Goodbye (when you are the one leaving).

감사합니다. [gam-sa-ham-ni-da.] / **고마워요.** [go-ma-wo-yo.] = Thank you.*

죄송합니다. [joe-song-ham-ni-da.] / **미안해요.** [mi-an-hae-yo.] = I'm sorry.*

얼마예요? [eol-ma-ye-yo?] = How much is it?

이거 주세요. [i-geo ju-se-yo.] = Please give this (one).

*Both expressions for each sentence can deliver the meaning, but the former words (with -**니다** [ni-da] at the end) are more formal, and the latter sound softer and less formal. You can use the formal words to someone who is older than you, and the less formal to someone obviously younger than you.

FOOD

RESTAURANT & CAFE

COMMON PHRASES

(item) + 주세요. [ju-se-yo]: Please give me (item).

The number of situations in which you can use 주세요 makes it the single most important phrase to know for survival in Korea. It is used in many everyday situations, especially in restaurants, bars, and cafes, but the simplest way to use it is by saying the item you would like, then add 주세요 at the end. 주세요 is also used in combination with verbs to request that someone do something for you.

Sample Sentences

김치찌개 주세요. [gim-chi-jji-gae ju-se-yo.] = Please give me kimchi stew.

카페 모카 **주세요**. [ka-pe mo-ka ju-se-yo.] = Please give me a café mocha.

숟가락 하나 더 **주세요**. [sut-kka-rak ha-na deo ju-se-yo.] = Please give me one more spoon.

이거 [i-geo] : this

If only using (item) + **주세요** [ju-se-yo] (please give me) makes it feel like you're not making yourself clear, you can use the word **이거** [i-geo]. By saying "**이거 주세요**" [i-geo ju-se-yo], you are saying, "please give me this" or "this one, please". Try pointing at a dish on the menu and saying "**이거 주세요**". The server will probably say the name of the dish for you to confirm, or say "**이거요**?" [i-geo-yo?], which means "oh, this one?", then you can answer with "**네**" [ne], meaning "yes".

Sample Sentences

이거 매워요? [i-geo mae-wo-yo.] = Is this spicy?

이거 주세요. [i-geo ju-se-yo.] = Please give me this one.

이거 맛있어요? [i-geo ma-si-sseo-yo?] = Is this good (delicious)?

Sample Dialogue

You: **이거** 주세요. [i-geo ju-se-yo.] = Please give me this.

Server: **이거요**? [i-geo-yo?] = This one?

You: **네**. [ne.] = Yes.

(item) + 있어요? [i-sseo-yo?] : Do you have (item)?

If you happen to know the name of the dish you want, and you happen to be at a restaurant that probably has it, you can try to order it by saying " name of the item + **있어요**?" [i-sseo-yo?], which literally means "does (item) exist?" or "do you have (item)?" For example, if you like **떡볶이** [tteok-ppo-kki], you can say, "**떡볶이 있어요**?" [tteok-ppo-kki i-sseo-yo?] If you also want **콜라** [kol-la], you can say, "**콜라 있어요**?" [kol-la i-sseo-yo?], meaning "do you have cola?" The server will either say "**있어요**" (we have it) or "**없어요**" [eop-sseo-yo] (we don't have it). He or she might also say something else, such as "**드릴까요**?" [deu-ril-kka-yo?] (shall we give you that?). Even if you don't understand exactly what he/she said to you, you can still understand if the restaurant has it or not through body language, tone of voice, or any other nonverbal communication from the waiter/waitress.

Sample Sentences

따뜻한 물 있어요? [tta-tteu-tan mul i-sseo-yo?] = Do you have warm water?

두유 라떼 있어요? [du-yu la-tte i-sseo-yo?] = Do you have soy milk latte?

포크 있어요? [po-keu i-sseo-yo?] = Do you have a fork?

저기요 [jeo-gi-yo]: excuse me

저기요 [jeo-gi-yo] is the phrase to use when you want to get the attention of servers at restaurants and cafes. Most of the time, servers won't come around to check if you need anything, and servers in Korea actually expect to be called over if customers need something. This sometimes requires saying "저기요" louder than the murmur of the restaurant patrons. It may be considered rude to speak so loudly in other parts of the world, but in Korea, at least when you are calling the server, it is common to say "저기요" loudly.

메뉴판 [me-nyu-pan]: the menu

If you want to ask for an English menu, you can say, "**영어 메뉴판**" [yeong-eo me-nyu-pan] or just "**영어 메뉴**" [yeong-eo me-nyu]. Many restaurants do not have a separate English menu, but you can always ask just in case.

At many Korean restaurants, the menus are written on the walls. When this is the case, it is usually written entirely in Korean. Additionally, some dishes at restaurants are only served in family-sized portions. There are usually Chinese characters (hanja) on the menus to denote the different sizes if this is the case.

소 [so] (小) - small (for 1-2 people)
중 [jung] (中) - medium (for 3-4 people)
대 [dae] (大) - large (for 5 or more people)

When spoken, **자** [ja] is added to the end of each size and pronounced as **짜** [jja].

메뉴판 [me-nyu-pan]: the menu

Sample Sentences

갈비찜 **소자** 주세요. [gal-bi-jjim so-jja ju-se-yo.] = *Please give me a small galbijjim.*

감자탕 **중자** 주세요. [gam-ja-tang jung-jja ju-se-yo.] = *Please give me a medium gamjatang.*

컵 [keop] : cup

The Korean pronunciation of "cup" is almost the same as English.

잔 [jan] : cup for alcohol

Typically you can use 컵 [keop] to refer to most cups, glasses, or mugs, but when it comes to drinking alcohol, the glass or cup is called 잔 [jan].

머그잔 [meo-geu-jan] = mug

This is a combination of the English word "mug" and the native Korean word for cup, 잔 [jan]. You may hear this at cafes when asked if you would like your drink in a mug rather than a disposable paper cup. In this case, you may hear "**머그잔으로 드릴까요**?" [meo-geu-jja-neu-ro deu-ril-kka-yo?] or "**머그잔에 드릴까요**?" [meo-geu-jja-ne deu-ril-kka-yo?] (shall I give it to you in a mug?) If you would like to ask for a mug instead of a paper cup, say "**머그잔으로 주세요**" [meo-geu-jja-neu-ro ju-se-yo] or "**머그잔에 주세요**" [meo-geu-jja-ne ju-se-yo] (please give it to me in a mug).

물 [mul] : water

Cultural tidbit: Koreans believe that drinking too much water before or during meals causes indigestion; therefore, many people typically drink water at the end of meals. There isn't anything culturally wrong with drinking water before or during meals, so don't feel pressured to not drink if you are thirsty!

Sample Sentences

물 한 잔 주세요. [mul han jan ju-se-yo.] = Please give me a glass of water.

뜨거운 물 주세요. [tteu-geo-un mul ju-se-yo.] = Please give me hot water.

얼음 물 주세요. [eu-reum mul ju-se-yo.] = Please give me ice water.

얼음 [eo-reum] : ice

Although the native Korean word for ice is 얼음 [eo-reum], 아이스 [a-i-seu], or the Korean pronunciation of the English word "ice", is also commonly used and understood.

냅킨 [naep-kin] : napkin

At most restaurants in Korea, the word 냅킨 [naep-kin] is understood. You can also request wet wipes, which are called 물티슈 [mul-ti-ssyu] in Korean. This literally translates to "water tissue".

드시고 가실 건가요? [deu-si-go ga-sil kkeon-ga-yo?] / 드시고 가세요? [deu-si-go ga-se-yo?]: For here (or to go)?

드시다 [deu-si-da] is an honorific form of the word, 먹다 [meok-tta] (to eat). The above phrases are literally asking if you will "eat and go", but are used to ask if your order is for here or to go. Since the servers are supposed to use polite and formal language when speaking to you as a customer, you will never hear "먹고 가실 건가요?" [meok-kko ga-sil kkeon-ga-yo?] or "먹고 가세요?" [meok-kko ga-se-yo?]

먹고 갈 거예요. [meo-kko gal kkeo-ye-yo.]: I'm drinking/eating here.

The literal translation of this phrase is "I will eat and go". Use this at cafes where orders are made upfront at the cashier so your order is prepared accordingly, which includes serving your coffee or tea in a mug rather than a disposable paper cup. Even though the server will use the verb "**드시다**" [deu-si-da] to mean "to drink" or "to eat", it is strange to use this verb about yourself, so always use "**먹다**" [meok-tta] (to eat/drink).

가지고 갈 거예요. [ga-ji-go gal kkeo-ye-yo.] / 테이크아웃 할게요. [te-i-keu-a-ut hal-kke-yo.]: I'm taking it out.

"Takeout" (**테이크아웃** [te-i-keu-a-ut]) is an English phrase that's also commonly used in Korean. This is more widely understood than the English phrase "to go" from "for here or to go". Use this word and the above phrases instead of the English phrase "to go".

영수증 [yeon-su-jeung]: receipt

Sample Sentences

영수증 드릴까요? [yeong-su-jeung deu-ril-kka-yo?] = Would you like a receipt?

영수증 버려 주세요. [yeong-su-jeung beo-ryeo ju-se-yo.] = Please throw the receipt away for me.

현금 영수증 [hyeon-geum yeong-su-jeung]: cash receipt

Cash receipts are used for tax purposes in Korea, and nearly all businesses will ask the following question when you're paying with cash. Although you may be asked, for most foreigners, it is not applicable.

Sample Sentences

현금 영수증 하시나요? [hyeon-geum yeong-su-jeung ha-si-na-yo?] = 현금 영수증 해 드릴까요? [hyeon-geum yeong-su-jeung hae deu-ril-kka-yo?] = Would you like the cash receipt?

싸인 [ssa-in] : signature

When paying with a credit or debit card, you will be asked to sign your receipt or sign on an electronic pad. If the transaction amount is lower than a certain amount, you might not be asked to sign anything. If that's the case, the cashier might say "싸인 안 하셔도 됩니다" [ssa-in an ha-syeo-do doem-ni-da]. Sometimes you may also hear the word 서명 [seo-myeong] instead of 싸인.

Sample Sentences

싸인 해 주세요. [ssa-in hae ju-se-yo.] = Sign please.

화장실 [hwa-jang-sil] : toilet

In busy shopping districts, in order to prevent too many passers-by from accessing the bathroom, some restaurants have customers pick up the keys to the bathroom from the counter, or there may be password locks on the bathroom doors. If there is a keypad on the door, be sure to check the receipt for a code!

Sample Sentences

여기 화장실이 어디에요? [yeo-gi hwa-jang-sil eo-di-e-yo?] = Where is the toilet (here in this place)?

You may hear:
2층에 있어요. [i-cheug-e i-sseo-yo.] = It is on the 2nd floor.
*층 [cheung] = floor

나가셔서 오른쪽에 있어요. [na-ga-syeo-seo o-reun-jjo-ge i-sseo-yo.] = Go out and to the right.

BREAK TIME

벨 (Bells)

At many restaurants, customers get the attention of the staff by saying "저기요" [jeo-gi-yo] (excuse me). When restaurants are loud, customers sometimes say "저기요" louder, which can still sometimes go unnoticed. To avoid this, at many restaurants (and bars), there are buttons on the table that ring a bell to signal to any available waitstaff that they are needed. Before shouting for the staff, look on the table to see if there is a button for a bell.

Tips

Korea is not a tipping culture, and it may even be confusing for staff to receive tips since they are not accustomed to receiving tips. Some Western-style bars have tips jars, but tips are usually not expected or are simply appreciated if received. Some servers might actually feel very uncomfortable when they receive a tip because they are already being paid salary, and receiving tips can feel like making money "on the side". However, at some upscale Western restaurants, tips are expected. These places are few and far between, but they do exist.

Utensils & Hidden Drawers

At many restaurants, utensils are in boxes on top of the table. When this is the case, customers are expected to set their own utensils. Sometimes, however, the utensil box may be neatly hidden away in a drawer underneath the table. If you can't find the utensils, remember to check under the table.

Paying the bill

Unlike in some cultures where restaurant staff will give you the bill at the end of the meal, in Korea, the bill is always at the table. Instead of handing your cash or credit card to the server to pay, customers are expected to take the bill to the front of the restaurant and pay for it on their way out. When you are finished with your meal, remember to take your bill to the front instead of handing your money to the server.

Side dishes

The side dishes, called 반찬 [ban-chan], that come with every Korean meal are free of charge and can be refilled at all times. If you don't know the name of a specific side dish, you can simply point and say "이거 더 주세요" [i-geo deo ju-se-yo], which means "please give me more of this". The main meal, however, is usually not refillable.

RESTAURANT

수저 : spoons and chopsticks

These are usually on the table already, either set up in front of you or in boxes, but in case you don't see them anywhere on your table, you will have to ask the servers. If you need a fork, the word is 포크 [po-keu].

반찬 [ban-chan] : side dishes

Side dishes are typically refillable for free, but more expensive items, such as meat, seafood, or fish, are not or may cost extra.

밥 [bap] : rice

밥 can refer to a "meal", but if you're in a restaurant and say 밥, you are specifically referring to steamed white rice.

(item) 빼 주세요. [(item) + ppae ju-se-yo.] : Please take out (item). / Please do not put in (item).
(고기) 안 먹어요. [(go-gi) an meo-geo-yo.] : I don't eat (meat).
(우유) 못 먹어요. [(u-yu) mon meo-geo-yo.] : I can't drink (milk).
(해물) 알레르기 있어요. [(hae-mul) al-le-reu-gi i-sseo-yo.] : I have an allergy (to seafood).

For those with allergies or aversions to certain foods, these are very useful phrases. Simply change out the words at the beginning to fit your dietary needs so that your orders are made to your liking. According to the dictionary, 안 refers to something you choose not to do, while 못 [mot] denotes something you are unable to do. When it comes to not eating something, most people use 못 (can't) because:

1) choosing not to eat a certain food may cause others inconvenience,

2) choosing not to eat something (especially if you have no allergy) is a relatively new concept in Korea.

Vegetarianism and veganism are on the rise in Korea, so you may find people saying "안 먹어요" [an meo-geo-yo] (I don't eat) more often in the future.

하나 더 주세요. [ha-na deo ju-se-yo.] : Give me one more of this.

If you really liked something and want to order one more, you can say this phrase. To be even clearer, you can add the name of the dish or 이거 [i-geo] (this) at the beginning of the phrase.

맥주 [maek-jju] : beer

Some restaurants may only have one type of beer, so if you just order **맥주**, they'll just bring whatever is available, which is usually a domestic Korean brand.

소주 [so-ju] : soju

Soju is stronger than beer, therefore it is sold in smaller bottles. Since soju bottles are smaller, the soju glasses are also quite small. You can pour roughly 7 glasses of soju from one bottle.

앞치마 [ap-chi-ma] : apron

Many restaurants offer aprons for customers so that clothes don't get stained. Not all restaurants in Korea have **앞치마**, but if you are grilling meat, cooking food at the table, or eating something with red ingredients (such as red pepper paste), aprons might be provided or available upon request.

For the same purpose, some places may offer giant plastic bags to protect your bags and other belongings from getting messy. A number of restaurants have booths with a "cubby" under the seat cushion or a cabinet under the table where you can place your items while you eat.

집게 [jip-kke] : tongs

In most meat restaurants, customers are expected to grill their own meat. Use the provided **집게** (and sometimes scissors) if you don't feel comfortable using the same chopsticks for both picking up raw meat and eating cooked meat. In some restaurants where the servers cook the meat for you, most of the time, he/she will only help you out in the beginning and sometimes cut the meat for you, but after that, the **집게** will be left on the table for you to continue cooking.

이쑤시개 [i-ssu-si-gae] : toothpick

Toothpicks are often found at the pay station. In regards to who uses toothpicks in Korea, it is rare to see any young person, especially a woman, use toothpicks. Realtively older people, most of the time men who do not feel embarrassed about using a toothpick in public, are often seen using toothpicks after meals.

사리 [sa-ri] : extra ingredients

Certain dishes can be ordered with extra ingredients. When you put these extra ingredients into a stew, it's referred to as **사리**. Although **사리** is often just noodles, it can also be rice cakes, cheese, eggs, sweet potato, and/or many others. Note that **사리** is different from **반찬** [ban-chan] (side dishes) since side dishes are served and eaten separately while **사리** is added to the stew during the cooking process.

공기 [gong-gi] : a counter for a bowl of rice

When ordering extra rice, "**공기밥**" [gong-gi-bap] is used. Since **밥** [bap] alone means "steamed rice", it is used together with the counter **공기**. When you want to order one bowl of steamed rice, you can say either "**공기밥 하나**" [gong-gi-bap ha-na] or "**밥 한 공기**" [ba pan-gong-gi].

쌈장 [ssam-jang] : condiment made from a mixture of red pepper paste and soybean paste

Ssamjang is a condiment that is reddish-brown in color because it is made by mixing **고추장** [go-chu-jang] (red pepper paste) and **된장** [doen-jang] (soybean paste) together with a few other ingredients. **쌈** [ssam] means "wrap", as in the vegetable or lettuce used to wrap cooked meat in, and **장** [jang] means "sauce"; therefore, **쌈장** is typically used on meat at a Korean barbecue restaurant. **쌈장** can also be used as a dipping sauce for vegetables.

뭐가 맛있어요? [mwo-ga ma-si-sseo-yo?] : What's good/delicious (here)? / What do you recommend?

This is a useful phrase for asking the waiter/waitress for a recommendation. Most restaurants have specialties and are able to suggest their most popular dishes or something that they can serve the quickest.

안 매운 거 있어요? [an mae-un geo i-sseo-yo?] : Do you have anything that's not spicy?

안 means "not", so if you are looking for a spicy dish, you can remove 안 from this phrase to ask if for anything that is spicy. "매운 거 있어요?" translates to "do you have anything spicy?"

판 갈아 주세요. [pan ga-ra ju-se-yo.] : Please change the grill grate.

Barbecue restaurants have grills at the tables, and the grill grates should be changed every so often to prevent food from burning. The grates, or more literally "pan" (판), can look like a flat frying pan or a steel net, depending on what type of meat you are cooking. "갈아 주세요" [ga-ra ju-se-yo] means "please change it", but only in the context of barbecue.

덜 맵게 해 주세요. [deol maep-kke hae ju-se-yo.] : Please make it less spicy.

덜 [deol] means "less", but if you would like your food to be made spicy, you can remove 덜 from this phrase to ask for a spicier version. "맵게 해 주세요" means "please make it spicy".

포장 돼요? [po-jang dwae yo?] : Do you pack for take-out?

포장 means "packaging" or "wrapping" and 돼요? means "is it doable?" or "is it possible?" To ask servers to pack your food for take out, you can use this phrase. If you want to just say, "please pack this (to go)" without asking if it's possible, you can simply say, "포장 해 주세요" [po-jang hae ju-se-yo] (please pack (this)).

앞접시 [ap-jjeop-ssi] : dish

Since many Korean foods are communal dishes, each person should have their own individual dish to put food into. 앞접시 literally means "front dish", and these are the dishes meant for individuals. Even if you are not given an 앞접시 by the servers, most restaurants will provide them if you ask.

The following are more words that can come in handy in a Korean restaurant.

More Words

콜라 [kol-la]	Coke (can be used to refer to most big name brown-colored sodas/fizzy drinks)
사이다 [sa-i-da]	Sprite (can also be used to refer to other clear sodas/fizzy drinks such as 7-Up or the popular Korean drink 칠성 사이다 [chil-sseong sa-i-da])
머스터드 [meo-seu-teo-deu]	mustard
케챱 [ke-chap]	ketchup
소금 [so-geum]	salt
후추 [hu-chu]	black pepper
상추 [sang-chu]	lettuce
참기름 [cham-gi-reum]	sesame oil
마늘 [ma-neul]	garlic

BREAK TIME

이모 [i-mo]
/ 아저씨 [a-jeo-ssi] / 저기요 [jeo-gi-yo] /
여기요 [yeo-gi-yo]

When calling over restaurant staff, different words are used depending on the person's sex and age. Older women are often referred to as 아줌마 [a-jum-ma], but this term implies older age. Instead, many women prefer to be called 이모 (auntie) since it is a more endearing term. 아저씨 [a-jeo-ssi] is acceptable for all ages of men. If you're ever unsure, just use the phrases "저기요" [jeo-gi-yo] or "여기요" [yeo-gi-yo], which are gender neutral.

Alcohol

Most Korean restaurants will serve only soju and/or domestic Korean beers, which are two of the most popular types of Korean alcohol and are sold everywhere. Other Korean alcohols, such as 막걸리 [mak-kkeol-li], 복분자주 [bok-ppun-ja-ju], 산사춘 [san-sa-chun], 백세주 [baek-sse-ju], etc. vary in level of popularity and are less common than soju and beer. Many times these liquors are sold for food pairing purposes. For example, 막걸리 is often consumed with 빈대떡 [bin-dae-tteok] (Korean-style pancakes) and is sold at these types of restaurants.

Different Types of Korean Alcohol

소주 [so-ju] is the most widely consumed alcohol in Korea. It tastes like a weaker vodka at 19% alcohol.

막걸리 [mak-kkeol-li] is a milky white rice wine that has an alcohol content ranging from 4% to 7%. The most common food pairing is with Korean mungbean pancake called 빈대떡 [bin-dae-tteok]. Also, 동동주 [dong-dong-ju] is very similar in taste and alcohol content.

산사춘 [san-sa-chun] is a medicinal alcohol that has a hint of red fruit from its fermentation process. It's a little sweet and has an alcohol content of 14%.

복분자주 [bok-ppun-ja] is a very sweet wine made from blackberries. It has an alcohol content ranging from 15% to 19%.

백세주 [baek-sse-ju] is another popular medicinal alcohol that has a nutty flavor. It has an alcohol content of 15% and costs about 8,000 won.

Smelly BBQ Clothes

Going to Korean barbecue restaurants can result in your clothes absorbing smoke and smelling like, well, grilled meat. Many restaurants now offer Febreze (페브리즈 [pe-beu-ri-jeu]) at the door to help you get rid of the smell. You may even be offered a giant plastic bag to put your jacket in once you sit down at a table to help protect it from the smell.

Who Grills the Meat?

At some BBQ restaurants, the staff will help grill the meat in the beginning. If they are too busy, however, you will have to do it yourself. In many restaurants, the servers will just bring you the meat so you can grill it yourself. Most of the time one person does the grilling and cutting. Sometimes people put meat on other people's plates when the pieces of meat are done cooking. If you're not the one grilling, consider taking over the grilling duties for your friend so s/he can eat, too!

CAFE

종이컵 [jong-i-kup] : paper cup

To ask for a paper cup instead of a mug, you can say, "**종이컵에 주세요**" [jong-i-keo-be ju-se-yo].

(휘핑) 크림 [(hwi-ping) keu-rim] : whipped cream

위에 (휘핑) 크림 얹어 드릴까요? [wi-e (whi-ping) keu-rim eon-jeo deu-ril-kka-yo?] (Do you want me to put some whipped cream on your drink?)
For certain drinks, such as café mocha, the staff will ask if you would like whipped cream on top. You can simply reply with "**네**" [ne] (yes) or "**아니요**"[a-ni-yo] (no).

(휘핑) 크림 빼 주세요. [(whi-ping) keu-rim ppae ju-se-yo] : Please don't put whipped cream (on top).

If you are not asked, you can use this phrase to ask for no whipped cream. (Item) + **빼 주세요** [(item) + ppae ju-se-yo] can be used for anything that you do not want in or on your beverage or food.

The following phrases are common in an exchange between customer and cashier when ordering drinks at a cafe:

사이즈 어떤 거 드릴까요? [ssa-i-jeu eo-tteon geo deu-ril-kka-yo?] : What size would you like?

Many cafes in Korea use the English words for sizes, but the smallest size is often called "tall" and a bigger size is often called "grande", which is similar to a very well-known and internationally recognized cafe chain. Although the words "small", "medium", and "large" are often used for other types of sizes (for example, regarding clothing), and are widely understood, these terms are not commonly used in cafes.

따뜻한 걸로 드릴까요 차가운 걸로 드릴까요? [tta-tteu-tan geol-lo deu-ril-kka-yo cha-ga-un geol-lo deu-ril-kka-yo?] : Would you like it hot or cold?

Answers:
따뜻한 거요. [tta-tteu-tan geo-yo] = Hot, please.
차가운 거요. [cha-ga-un geo-yo] = Cold, please.

음료 나오면 진동벨로 알려드릴게요. [eum-ryo na-o-myeon jin-dong-bel-lo al-lyeo deu-ril-kke-yo.] : When your drink is ready, we will let you know through the pager.

Most larger cafe chains in Korea will give patrons a pager that signals when an order is ready. Most pagers just light up and vibrate, but some have a screen that shows advertisements, which unfortunately cannot be turned off manually.

오른쪽에서 바로 준비해 드릴게요. [o-reun-jjo-ge-seo ba-ro jun-bi-hae deu-ril-kke-yo.] : We will prepare your beverage right away over there to the right.

If you order something that can be prepared very quickly, such as bottled juice or a canned soft drink, the staff will direct you to the other end of the counter where your order will be given promptly. If it's to the right side, someone will say "오른쪽" [o-reun-jjok], and if it's to the left, it's "왼쪽" [oen-jjok]. Either way, you will be pointed in the general direction and it will be pretty clear as to where you can pick up your order.

데워 주세요. [de-wo ju-se-yo] : Please heat it up.

If you order things that might need a quick heat up in the microwave, the staff might ask you 데워 드릴까요? [de-wo deu-ril-kka-yo?] before you have the chance to ask. To respond to this, you can simply say 네 [ne]. If they don't ask, you can ask them using this sentence. For example, if you want to ask them to heat up your muffin, you can say, "머핀 데워 주세요" [meo-pin de-wo ju-se-yo] (heat it up, please).

두유 [du-yu] : soymilk

두유로 주세요. [du-yu-ro ju-se-yo.] : Please make it with soymilk.

Most major cafes chains will have soymilk, but not every cafe in Korea has it.

무릎 담요 [mu-reup dam-nyo] : lap blanket

Lap blankets will keep you warm, but in Korea, they are also used to cover short skits and prevent any embarassing moments. If a cafe is drafty, or there is a place where people can sit on the floor, lap blankets are readily available. On the other hand, if there are primarily tables and chairs that are high off the ground, the chances of getting a lap blanket are pretty slim.

Sample Sentences

여기 무릎 담요 있어요? [yeo-gi mu-reup dam-nyo iss-eo-yo?] = Do you have a lap blanket?

무릎 담요 좀 주세요 [mu-reup dam-nyo jom ju-se-yo.] = Plesae give me a lap blankeet.

47

와이파이 [wa-i-pa-i] : Wi-Fi

와이파이 돼요? [wa-i-pa-i dwae-yo?] : Is Wi-Fi available here?

Many cafes in Korea have free Wi-Fi for customers, but some retail chains will only offer Wi-Fi for customers with cell service through particular carriers such as KT Olleh, LG U+, or SK Telecom. The English word "wireless" is not commonly understood, so be sure to say "Wi-Fi"!

와이파이 비밀번호 뭐예요? [wa-i-pa-i bi-mil-beo-no mwo-ye-yo?] : What's the Wi-Fi password?

Some cafes will have their Wi-Fi signals locked so that only they can allow their customers to use the wireless connection. Some cafes will have the Wi-Fi password printed on the receipt, and some will have it written on the wall or at the counter. Since it's fast becoming a norm for cafes to provide customers with wireless Internet connection, you can almost always rely on the cafe providing a fast Wi-Fi connection.

Here are the names of some popular beverages and snacks that are relatively easy to remember. Many of them are actually Konglish words, which are just English words written in Korean and pronounced with a Korean accent.

More Words

아메리카노 [a-me-ri-ka-no]	café americano; long black
에스프레소 [e-seu-peu-re-sso]	espresso
카페 모카 [ka-pe mo-ka]	café mocha
카페 라떼 [ka-pe la-tte]	café latte
카푸치노 [ka-pu-chi-no]	cappuccino
핫초코 [hat-cho-ko]	hot chocolate
레몬차 [le-mon-cha]	lemon tea
녹차 [nok-cha]	green tea
머핀 [meo-pin]	muffin
샌드위치 [saen-deu-wi-chi]	sandwich
케이크 [ke-i-keu]	cake

Sample Dialogue

Clerk: 주문하시겠어요? [ju-mun-ha-si-ge-sseo-yo?] = Would you like to order?

Customer: 카페라떼 하나 주세요. [ka-pe-la-tte ha-na ju-se-yo.] = Café latte, please.

Clerk: 머그잔으로 드릴까요? [meo-geu-ja-neu-ro deu-ril-kka-yo?] = Shall I put it in a mug?

Customer: 네. [ne.]/아니요, 테이크 아웃 잔에 주세요. [a-ni-yo, te-i-keu a-ut ja-ne ju-se-yo.] = Yes./No, I'd like to get it to go.

Clerk: 여기서 드실 건가요? [yeo-gi-seo deu-sil kkeon-ga-yo?]= For here (or to go)?

Customer: 네. [ne.]/아니요. [a-ni-yo.] = Yes./No.

Clerk: 4,300원입니다. [sa-cheon-sam-bae-gwo-nim-ni-da.] = That's 4,300 won.

Customer: (hands cash / card)

Clerk: 현금 영수증 드릴까요? [hyeon-geum yeong-su-jeung deu-ril-kka-yo?]/ 여기 싸인해 주세요. [yeo-gi ssa-in-hae ju-se-yo.] = Do you want the cash receipt?/Please sign here please.

Customer: 아니요. [a-ni-yo.]/(signs) = No.

Clerk: 음료 나오면 진동벨로 알려드릴게요. [eum-ryo na-o-myeon jin-dong-bel-lo al-lyeo deu-ril-ge-yo.] = You will know when your drink is ready when your pager goes off.

BREAK TIME

Phone charging

Most cafes in Korea will charge phones for free if there happens to be compatible cables for a specific type of phone available. Since it is becoming more and more common for cafes to deliberately prepare various types of cables for both Android and Apple phones for the satisfaction and convenience of customers, if you don't have a charging cable with you, you can try asking at the counter if there is one available by saying, "충전할 수 있나요?" [chung-jeo-nal su in-na-yo?] Even if you don't say the entire phrase, you will be understood the moment you say the word 충전 [chung-jeon], which means "recharging".

If you have your phone charger with you and see a wall outlet near you, you can simply charge it yourself.

FOOD
DELIVERY

여기(address) + -인데 (menu item) + - 배달해 주세요.

[yeo-gi (address) + in-de (menu item) + bae-da-rae ju-se-yo.] : **Please deliver (menu item) to (address).**

This phrase combines the two most essential parts of food delivery: address and order. It's everything needed for ordering delivery over the phone. Often times, when you order food by telephone, the other person on the phone (the business) expects you to say this right away after he/she answers the phone and greets you. In some situations, however, you may be asked preemptively for your address or order before you've had a chance to speak.

Sample Sentences

여기 한국 아파트인데 치킨 한 마리 **배달해 주세요.** [yeo-gi han-guk a-pa-teu-in-de chi-kin han ma-ri bae-da-rae ju-se-yo.] = I'm here at HanGuk Apartments. Please deliver one order of chicken.

여기 연희동 123-4567인데 김치찌개 3인분 **배달해 주세요.** [yeo-gi yeon-hui-dong il-i-sam-da-si-sa-o-yuk-chi-rin-de gim-chi-jji-gae sa-min-bun bae-da-rae ju-se-yo.] = I'm here at Yeonhui-dong 123-4567. Would you please deliver three servings of kimchi jjigae?

여기 한국 빌라 1동 2호인데 페페로니 피자 세 판 **배달해 주세요.** [yeo-gi han-guk bil-la il-dong i-ho-in-de pe-pe-ro-ni pi-ja se pan bae-da-rae ju-se-yo.] = I'm at HanGuk Villa 1-dong, 2-ho. Would you please deliver three pepperoni pizzas?

To ask for your address, someone might say:

주소가 어떻게 되세요? [ju-so-ga eo-tteo-ke doe-se-yo?] : **What is your address?**

어디세요? [eo-di-se-yo] : **Where are you? (asking for address)**

In Korea, addresses are written and said from general to specific in this order: city, ward, neighborhood, building number, apartment/room number. Since the majority of delivery serivces are typically nearby, you only need to state the neighborhood, building number, and apartment/room number, as 구 and 시 are unnecessary.

Tips:
- A hyphen in Korean is read as "dash" (**다시** [da-si]). For example: 220-65 (**이백이십 다시 육십오** [i-bae-gi-sip da-si yuk-ssi-bo])
- If you live in a large building that has a name, like Viva Family Apartments, Daewoo officetel, etc., delivery places will know the building name if they are in the local area. You just can state your building name along with your apartment number.
- Some places will save your phone number so that you don't have to repeat your address each time you call.
- The new address system in Korea took effect in January of 2014 and uses road names rather than building numbers. Be sure to check your address in both the old and new systems.

여기 + (neighborhood) + –인데 – 배달 돼요? [yeo-gi (neighborhood) + in-de bae-dal dwae-yo?] : I'm here at (neighborhood), do you deliver?

When calling for delivery, it's common to ask if the place will deliver to where you are by stating the name of your neighborhood. Say your neighborhood first (it doesn't have to be the full address) by saying "**여기** (neighborhood) **인데**", "I'm here at (address)". Finish the sentence by asking if they deliver with "**배달 돼요?**"

뭘로 드릴까요? [mwol-lo deu-ril-kka-yo?] : What can I get you?

Respond by stating your order in this fashion: (food order) + (number and/or size) + **주세요.** [ju-se-yo.]

Sample Sentences

치킨 한 마리 **주세요.** [chi-kin han ma-ri ju-se-yo.] = Please give me one (order of) chicken.
페페로니 피자 세 판 **주세요.** [pe-pe-ro-ni pi-ja se pan ju-se-yo.] = Please give me three pepperoni

pizzas.

* Note that ordering requires the use of counters. See "counters" at the end of this chapter.

카드로 계산할게요. [ka-deu-ro gye-san-hal-kke-yo.] : I will pay with my card.
카드 돼요? [ka-deu dwae-yo?] : Can I pay with my card?

Nearly all food delivery accepts credit cards, but be sure to mention it on the phone so that they remember to bring the credit card reader. If you don't mention it while placing your order and the delivery driver doesn't bring the credit card reader, he/she will have to come back again to collect the payment.

Sample Dialogue

You: 여기 망원동인데 배달 돼요? [yeo-gi mang-won-dong-in-de bae-dal dwae-yo?] = I'm here at Mangwon-dong. Do you deliver?

Delivery: 네. [ne.] 주소가 어떻게 되세요? [ju-so-ga eo-tteo-ke doe-se-yo?] = Yes. What's your address?

You: 망원동 망원 빌라 가동 123호요. [mang-won-dong mang-won bil-la ga-dong il-i-sam-ho-yo.] = Mangwon-dong, Mangwon Villa Ga-dong 123-ho.

Delivery: 뭘로 드릴까요? [mwol-lo deu-ril-kka-yo?] = What can I get you?

You: 김치찌개 하나랑 김밥 세 줄 주세요. [gim-chi-jji-gae ha-na-rang gim-ppap se jul ju-se-yo.] = Please give me one kimchi jjigae and three rolls of gimbap.

Delivery: 네. [ne.] 김치찌개 하나랑 김밥 세 줄이요. [gim-chi-jji-gae ha-na-rang gim-ppap se ju-ri-yo.] = Okay. One kimchi jjigae and three rolls of gimbap.

You: 얼마예요? [eol-ma-ye-yo?] = How much is it?

Delivery: 만원입니다. [ma-nwo-nim-ni-da.] = That will be 10,000 won.

You: 카드 되나요? [ka-deu doe-na-yo?] = Do you take cards?

Delivery: 네./아니요. [ne.]/[a-ni-yo.] = Yes./No.

얼마나 걸려요? [eol-ma-na geol-lyeo-yo?] : How long will it take?

You can ask how long it will take and the place will tell you if they think it will take longer than usual.

(time) + - 분/시간 전에 주문했는데 아직 안 왔어요. [(time) + bun/si-gan jeo-ne ju-mun-haen-neun-de a-jik an wa-sseo-yo.] : I ordered it (time) ago, but I haven't received it yet.

Most food delivery in Korea is fairly quick. If you've been waiting for more than 40 minutes, you may want to call to make sure they processed your order correctly. 분 means "minute" and 시간 means "hour" or "time".

Sample Sentences

1시간 전에 주문했는데 아직 안 왔어요. [han-si-gan jeo-ne ju-mun-haen-neun-de a-jik an wa-sseo-yo.] = I ordered it an hour ago, but I haven't received it yet.

50분 전에 주문했는데 아직 안 왔어요. [o-sip-ppun jeo-ne ju-mun-haen-neun-de a-jik an wa-sseo-yo.] = I ordered it 50 minutes ago, but I haven't received it yet.

출발했나요? [chul-bal-haen-na-yo?] : Has the delivery person left?

When calling back to ask the whereabouts of your food, you can ask if the delivery person has left to deliver your order. Many times you may hear "금방 갈게요" [geum-bang gal-kke-yo], which means "we'll be there shortly".

다 드시고 그릇은 문 앞에 놓아 주세요. [da deu-si-go geu-reu-seun mu-na-pe no-a ju-se-yo.] : Please leave the dishes in front of your door after you finish eating.

As an alternative to disposable dishes and packaging, many restaurants deliver food on regular plates and bowls used in their restaurants. If you receive non-disposable dishes and/or utensils, the delivery person may say this phrase to remind you to give their dishes back.

숟가락 [sut-kka-rak] : spoon / 젓가락 [jeot-kka-rak] : chopsticks / 수저 [su-jeo] : spoon and chopsticks

Restaurants will provide you with spoons and chopsticks, usually disposable ones, but sometimes you'll get actual metal utensils. You may be asked if you need utensils just in case you prefer to use your own.

단무지 [dan-mu-ji] : pickled radish

Pickled radish is a side dish that comes with any Korean-Chinese food delivery, the most common delivery food in Korea. It also comes with 생양파 [saeng-yang-pa], raw onions, and 춘장 [chun-jang], black dipping sauce.

콜라 [kol-la] : Coke / 사이다 [sa-i-da] : cider (Sprite/7up)

The citrusy carbonated drink, similar to Sprite or 7up, is called "사이다" in Korea and usually refers to a Korean brand 칠성 사이다 [chil-sseong sa-i-da].

양념 반 후라이드 반 [yang-nyeom ban hu-ra-i-deu ban] : half sweet and sour chicken and half fried chicken

Fried chicken is one of Korea's most popular delivery foods with the top two types being plain fried chicken and marinated sweet and sour chicken. 양념 반 후라이드 반 is half fried chicken and half marinated sweet and sour chicken. Instead of using the full expression 양념 반 후라이드 반, you can also just say 반반 [ban-ban], which means "half-half".

쿠폰 [ku-pon] : coupon

Many delivery places will offer loyalty rewards with coupons (i.e. buy 10, get next one free). These are often found on chicken or pizza boxes, on take out menus, or the driver will simply just hand the coupon to you.

BREAK TIME

Counters

When ordering food, you will need to indicate how many you would like to order. Depending on what you are ordering, you will have to use different "counters" which are special Korean counting words.

피자 한 판 [pi-ja han pan] = one pizza
(두 판, 세 판 …)

판 [pan] is the counter for pizza pies. For pizzas, you should also indicate size which are the same in Korean as English (**미디엄** [mi-di-eom] = medium, **라지** [la-ji] = large, **레귤러** [le-gyul-leo] = regular).

치킨 한 마리 [chi-kin han ma-ri] = one order of chicken
(두 마리, 세 마리 …)

마리 [ma-ri] is a counter for animals. For delivery, you will use this mostly for fried chicken.

짜장면 한 그릇 [jja-jang-myeon han geu-reut] = one serving of Chinese black bean sauce noodles
(두 그릇, 세 그릇 …)

그릇 [geu-reut] is a counter for bowls and is often used for Chinese food delivery.

김치찌개 한 개 / 하나 [gim-chi-jji-gae han-gae/ha-na] = one order of kimchi stew
(한 개, 두 개, 세 개)

개 [gae] is a general counter for anything else and can be used for general Korean food orders. For one serving, you can just say "**하나**", which is the native Korean number for "one" because it does not need a counter. For two or more servings, it's more natural to order with using the counter **개**.

Wherever You Are	Delivery in Korea isn't limited to home or office addresses. Many places will also deliver to outdoor locations such as parks or university campuses. Explaining your location may be more difficult as you'll have to explain in detail where you are (e.g. next to the baseball field, under the tree, under the bridge, etc.)
Neighborhood Delivery Pamphlets	If you enjoy delivery, look for delivery pamphlets which can be found in apartment buildings. These pamphlets are sometimes placed on your door handle each month or there may be an area in the main lobby where people will leave various advertisements for local restaurants. The pamphlets will have phone numbers and menu items for many of the local delivery businesses all in one booklet. Some booklets also have coupons that can be collected (10 coupons = free dish).
Popular Delivery Foods	Chinese food (**중국요리** [jung-gung-yo-ri]) is one of the most popular delivery foods. It's found in every corner of Korea and is one of the cheapest eats. The two most common dishes are **짜장면** [jja-jang-myeon], a noodle dish with black bean sauce, and **짬뽕** [jjam-ppong], a spicy, bright red seafood noodle dish. Fried Chicken (**치킨** [chi-kin]) is another popular delivery food in Korea, and it comes in several varieties: fried, marinated, garlic, soy sauce, etc. Bossam (**보쌈** [bo-ssam]) is boiled pork belly slices with vegetable wraps and is a common delivery food. It is best enjoyed with a bottle of **소주** [so-ju]. Jokbal (**족발** [jok-ppal]) is sliced trotter (pig feet) and another pork dish with vegetable wraps that's best enjoyed with a bottle of alcohol.

TRANS-
POR-
TATION

BUS & SUBWAY

COMMON PHRASES

교통 카드 [gyo-tong ka-deu] : transportation card

Transportation cards are convenient prepaid cards that allow you to use public transportation without having to pay with cash each time you want to use the bus or subway. In addition to being super convenient, transportation cards offer discounts and free transfers to and from buses and subways. The card itself can be purchased with or without any credit on it, usually at subway stations or convenience stores. Just load the card with money and the funds will be deducted each time you take a ride. The card keeps track of the money for you, so you will always have a good idea how much money you have left on your card if you look at the bottom number on the sensor where you place your card when you get on or off a bus or subway.

In Seoul, bus-to-bus, bus-to-subway, or subway-to-bus transfers are free of charge if it's within 30 minutes. (However, subway-to-subway transfer is not free once you tap out at a subway station.)

충전 [chung-jeon] : recharging; refilling (one's card)

충전해 주세요. [chung-jeon-hae ju-se-yo.] : Please charge my card.

After purchasing a transportation card, funds must be added before you can use it to ride a bus or take the subway. You can add money at most convenience stores (GS25, 7-11, Family Mart, Mini Stop, etc.) by using this phrase. You can include the amount of credit you want to add before saying "충전해 주세요".

Sample Sentences

오천 원 충전해 주세요. [o-cheo-nwon chung-jeon-hae ju-se-yo.] = Please add 5,000 won to my card.

만 원 충전해 주세요. [ma-nwon chung-jeon-hae ju-se-yo.] = Please add 10,000 won to my card.

If you are at a subway station, there are "Ticket and Card Reloading" machines where you can recharge your card. These machines have instructions in several languages, so just select your preferred language and follow the on-screen instructions.

노약자석 [no-yak-jja-seok] : priority seating

Priority seating is labeled accordingly on buses and the subway. Just like in many countries, these seats are reserved for the elderly, disabled, expecting mothers, or mothers with small children.

앉으세요. [an-jeu-se-yo.] : Please sit.

Use this phrase when giving up your seat for an elderly person or a pregnant woman. In Korea, it is common for passengers to offer their seats to little children who may have a difficult time standing while the bus or subway is running.

환승 [hwan-seung] : transfer

환승입니다. [hwan-seung-im-ni-da.] = (You are) Transferring.

If you use a transportation card to transfer from bus to subway, or vice versa, within 30 minutes, the sensor machines on buses and at subway stations will say this phrase. It is meant to alert the traveler that the free transfer has been successfully registered and that no extra funds have been charged.

잔액이 부족합니다. [ja-nae-gi bu-jo-kam-ni-da.] : You have insufficient funds.

When your transportation card doesn't have enough funds for the trip, the machine will say this phrase. If you hear the machine say this phrase on a bus, you will have to use a different card or pay in cash (don't forget to get your change from the driver if you do pay with cash).

잠시만요. [jam-si-man-nyo.] : Excuse me.

When a bus or subway is crowded and you're tying to make your way to the door, use this phrase to tell other passengers that you'll be getting off.

첫차 [cheot-cha]: first train/bus
막차 [mak-cha]: last train/bus

첫차 몇 시예요? [cheot-cha myeot ssi-ye-yo?] = When is the first train/bus?

막차 몇 시예요? [mak-cha myeot ssi-ye-yo?] = When is the last train/bus?

Unfortunately, most public transportation does not run 24 hours. Final runs for subway stations and buses all differ, but generally, public transportation stops running around 11:30 p.m. Some go as late as 1 a.m. but start operating again around 5 a.m. Use these two phrases to ask someone about the first or last bus or train. The information on the running hours is usually written at every bus stop and subway station, but typically only in Korean.

BREAK TIME

Transportation Cards

If you plan on using public transportation, you may want to consider getting a transportation card. Instead of stopping to pay each time you get on, transportation cards allows you to pay a larger amount upfront so every time you pay for a ride, the fare is automatically deducted. The base fares are ₩100 cheaper with a transportation card than if you pay with cash. Transfers between buses and subways within 30 minutes are free or discounted, and cards can also used for taxi rides, convenience stores, vending machines, and other businesses.

Korea makes it very easy to carry a transportation card since you can get them in all shapes and sizes. The most common are in the form of a typical plastic card that's the same size and shape of a credit card so it fits in a wallet. There are more stylish cards that double as phone charms or key chains, while some mobile phones have transportation card-enabled SIM cards. Bank cards also have the ability to be used as transportation cards. Different regions can have their own transportation cards, but the two main brands are "T-money" and "Cashbee", which cover most of the major cities in Korea.

Priority Seats

Just as in other countries, priority seats, 노약자석 [no-yak-jja-seok] in Korean, are reserved for elderly, disabled, and pregnant people. However, in Korea, there's an unwritten rule that those reserved seats are to ONLY be used by the aforementioned. If the only seats available are the priority seats, the majority of able-bodied people will stand, although people can sit in these seats and just get up when someone in need comes into the train. It is not common, however, for priority seats to be open, especially during rush hour.

Transportation Costs

All public transportation fares have a minimum cost which can differ depending on the city. For example, as of September 2015, the base subway fare in Seoul is ₩1,350 and ₩1,300 in Busan. If you use a transportation card however, the minimum fare is reduced by ₩100 to ₩1,250 and ₩1,200, respectively. These minimum fares cover a specified distance (usually 10km), and the fare increases the further you travel. For single-use cards, your full fare should be paid for, but for prepaid transportation cards, the initial minimum fare is deducted at the entry gate and additional charges will be deducted at the exit gate.

BUS

(place) + 가요? [(place) ga-yo?] : Does this bus go to (place)?

Buses have destinations written on the side panel of the bus that faces the sidewalk. The bus routes can be found at every bus stop, but only in Korean. If you're unsure if a bus goes to a certain destination, you can ask the driver using this phrase before getting on. Change the destination at the beginning of this phrase to fit your needs.

Sample Sentences

홍대입구역 **가요?** [hong-dae-ip-kku-yeok ga-yo?] = (Does this bus) go to Hongik University station?

광화문 **가요?** [gwang-hwa-mun ga-yo?] = (Does this bus) go to Gwanghwamun?

시청 **가요?** [si-cheong ga-yo?] = (Does this bus) go to City Hall?

(number of people) + 명이요. [(number of people) + myeong-i-yo.] : I'm paying for ... people.

On buses, you can pay for several passengers with a single transportation card. Before putting your card on the sensor upon boarding, tell the driver if you are paying for more

people than just yourself. The driver will adjust the fare accordingly and you will be on your way. If you transfer to the subway after paying for multiple people on the bus, you will not get a free transfer since everyone needs an individual card or ticket to use the subway.

*– 명 [myeong] is a counter for people

Sample Sentences

두 **명이요.** [du myeong-i-yo.] = Please charge for two people on this card.

세 **명이요.** [se myeong-i-yo.] = Please charge for three people on this card.

(amount of money) + 원 냈어요. [(amount of money) + won nae-sseo-yo.] : I paid ....

Buses have a clear box for cash payments. Since the cash is not going directly into the hands of the driver, the driver may not see the exact amount that you paid. If you need change, tell the bus driver the exact amount that was paid, and you should get your change back. Since all your change will be in coins, it is best not to pay in anything other than ₩1,000 bills. It is very common to see people pay ₩2,000 and ask for change, but it is not as common to see people paying with a ₩5,000 or ₩10,000 bill and receive the entire change amount in coins.

Sample Sentences

천원 **냈어요.** [cheo-nwon nae-sseo-yo.] = I paid ₩1,000.

2천원 **냈어요.** [i-cheo-nwon nae-sseo-yo.] = I paid ₩2,000.

정류장 [jeong-ryu-jang] / 정거장 [jeong-geo-jang] : (bus/subway) stop

이번 정류장은 …입니다. [i-beon jeong-ryu-jang-eun... im-ni-da.] = This stop is ....

다음 정류장은 …입니다. [da-eum jeong-ryu-jang-eun... im-ni-da.] = The next stop is ....

Bus/subway stops are announced inside the bus/subway through automated announcements. Although there are announcements in other languages for select bus stops, the majority are announced in Korean and knowing these phrases is useful for getting around on public transportation. The most important thing is to know how to differentiate between **이번** [i-beon] and **다음** [da-eum], because **이번** means "this time" and **다음** means "next". Many people make the mistake of getting off at a bus stop as soon as they hear the name of their stop, then realize it was going to be the "next" stop.

승차 [seung-cha] : getting on the vehicle
하차 [ha-cha] : getting off the vehicle

승차 하실 때 교통카드를 단말기에 대 주세요. [seung-cha ha-sil ttae gyo-tong-ka-deu-reul dan-mal-gi-e dae ju-se-yo.] : Please place your transportation card on the card reader when you get on the bus.

하차 하실 때도 교통 카드를 단말기에 접촉하셔야 추가 요금이 나오지 않습니다. [ha-cha ha-sil ttae-do gyo-tong ka-deu-reul dan-mal-gi-e jeop-cho-ka-syeo-ya chu-ga yo-geu-mi na-o-ji an-sseum-ni-da.] : You have to place your transportation card on the card reader in order to avoid any extra charges.

하차 하실 때도 교통 카드를 단말기에 접촉하셔야 환승 할인이 적용됩니다. [ha-cha ha-sil ttae-do gyo-tong ka-deu-reul dan-mal-gi-e jeop-cho-ka-syeo-ya hwan-seung ha-ri-ni jeo-gyong-doem-ni-da.] : You have to place your transportation card on the card reader in order to get the transfer discount.

These are automated announcements you may hear on the bus which remind passengers to place transportation cards on the sensors. Transportation cards should be read upon entering and exiting the bus. If you forget to put your card on the reader upon exiting, the free transfer is forfeited and the price of the transfer is added onto your next ride on the bus or subway.

For instance, your initial bus ride is ₩1,200. You transfer to a second bus within 30 minutes of getting off the initial bus. When you get off the second bus, you forget to put your card on the sensor. The next time you take a bus or train ride, you will be charged for the transfer between buses PLUS the ride you are about to take.

If you are not going to transfer to another bus or to the subway within 30 minutes, or within 1 hour between 9 p.m. and 7 a.m., you don't have to bother thinking about this.

문 열어 주세요. [mun yeo-reo ju- se -yo.] : **Please open the door.**

Sometimes bus drivers will close doors too quickly before you've had a chance to get off, or you might have suddenly realized at the last minute that this is your stop. In either case, you can use this phrase to ask the driver to open the door again. If no one presses the buzzer which indicates wanting to get off at the upcoming stop, the driver might stop by the bus stop, but not open the door. If you missed your chance to press the buzzer in time, you can say "문 열어 주세요" or "내릴게요" [nae-ril-kke-yo] (I'm getting off, so please open the back door.).

벨 [bel] : **bell, buzzer**

Although buttons are located throughout the bus, many buses also have buttons on the ceilings. If you're trying to ring the 벨 on a crowded bus, the closest button to you may be on the ceiling, so be sure to look up! The 벨 are not lit up by default, so if all the 벨 on the bus are lit up, it means that someone has already pushed the 벨 for the upcoming stop.

심야 버스 [si-mya ppeo-sseu] : night bus

Night buses, called **심야 버스** in Korean, were introduced in Seoul in late 2013. These buses are marked with an "N" as well as clever owl symbol. **심야 버스** run from midnight until 5 a.m. and are found in places where there tend to be many people late at night, such as Hongdae and Gangnam.

심야 버스 [si-mya ppeo-sseu] : night bus

BREAK TIME

**Getting Off
The Bus**

Most bus drivers in Korea expect passengers to be waiting at the back door before the bus comes to a complete stop. That means most passengers walk toward the back door while the bus is still in motion in order to get off. If you wait in your seat until the bus comes to a complete stop, the bus driver may assume that no one is getting off and continue on. This is a bit of a safety problem, so some bus drivers make an effort to wait a little longer at each stop with the door open to make sure everyone gets off safely. However, since the buses are on a schedule, the majority of bus drivers do not waste time at bus stops.

**Types of buses
in Seoul**

If you're traveling in Seoul, the city bus system has color-coded buses which denote the destination and route.

Village bus
마을 버스 [ma-eul ppeo-sseu] (village bus) are green, but they are not the same as the green buses in downtown areas. These buses will ferry commuters within a small geographic area, usually to and from areas with non-major roads. Traveling short distances makes the price of this bus cheaper than other types of buses. Village buses are smaller in comparison to the other buses listed below, making them easy to identify.

Green bus
This city bus is used to connect subway stations and major bus depots in downtown Seoul.

Blue bus
These are "regular" city buses that travel on major roads and stop at major bus stops. Green and blue buses can share bus stops, so it's not uncommon to see a blue bus and a green bus at the same stop.

Red bus
광역 버스 [gwang-yeok ppeo-sseu], or red buses, are express busses that travel

from one city to another and stop at fewer locations than a green or a blue bus. If your destination or starting point is outside of Seoul, these express buses may be faster than taking a train or the subway.

Yellow bus
The yellow buses are quite elusive. They do exist, but because these buses basically travel in a circle within major district areas, such as Gangnam, it is rare if you are able to see or ride one of these buses.

Airport limousines buses
These buses are known as **공항 버스** [gong-hang ppeo-seu] in Korean and have routes that travel from Incheon or Gimpo Airport to nearly every corner of Seoul and every city throughout the country.

SUBWAY

(Station Name) + 역 [(station name) yeok] : ... station

This is one of the most essential words for surviving in Korea and one of the first words learned by those that come to live in Korea. It is used in regards to navigating subway routes, but subway stations are also used when directing taxi drivers to a certain destination. Additionally, subway stations are used as meeting points and as reference points when giving directions.

Sample Sentences

이번 역 [i-beon nyeok] = this station/stop

다음 역 [da-eum nyeok] = next station/stop

무슨 역에서 내려야 돼요? [mu-seun nyeo-ge-seo nae-ryeo-ya dwae-yo?] = Which station do we have to get off at?

이태원역 [i-tae-won-yeok] = Itaewon Station

강남역 [gang-nam-nyeok] = Gangnam Station

교대역 [gyo-dae-yeok] = Seoul National University of Education Station

서울역 [seo-ul-lyeok] = Seoul Station

~호선 [ho-seon] / ~선 [seon] : line

When referring to subway lines, you'll need to add either 호선 or 선 to the line you are talking about. Subway lines that are numbered from 1 to 9 have 호선 following the number (i.e. 4호선 [sa-ho-seon]). For subway lines with names, 선 is added to the names (중앙선 [jung-ang-seon]).

Sample Sentences

1호선 [i-ro-seon] = Line 1
9호선 [gu-ho-seon] = Line 9
분당선 [bung-dang-seon] = Bundang Line

(station name) + 방면 [(station name) + bang-myeon] : (station name) bound
(station name) + 행 [(station name) + haeng] : (station name) bound

You will see or hear these messages on subway announcements. Both are useful for confirming that you are traveling in the right direction.

갈아타는 곳 [ga-ra-ta-neun got] : transfer point

Transferring between subway lines is free of charge. Some stations have transfer gates where transportation cards must be put up against the card readers. These transfer gates do not charge any additional fares.

⋯번 출구 [beon chul-gu] : Exit (number)...

Directions in Korea are often given in relation to subway stations and their exit numbers (i.e. first right out of exit 3, Gangnam Station). Subway station exits are also often used as meeting points.

Some subway stations are very large and have multiple exits that seem miles away from each other. Each exit is marked with a number

Sample Sentences

3번 출구 [sam-beon chul-gu] = Exit 3
5번 출구 [o-beon chul-gu] = Exit 5

급행 [geu-paeng] : Express
일반 [il-ban] : All-stop (local)

Most subways lines are local trains, making stops at every station. However, a few selected lines in Seoul have express trains. Be sure to confirm which train you should take to reach your destination.

BREAK TIME

Buying a ticket (Single Use)

If you're not using a transportation card, you must purchase a ticket at the machines found in each station. The machines have language options in Korean, English, Japanese, and Chinese. Just choose your destination and pay the amount. You are then required to give a ₩500 deposit for a single use card which can be refunded at the destination station from the deposit refund machines. If, however, in the middle of your ride, you decide to change destinations, the fare you pay may be higher than what you originally paid. If this is the case, you will have to deposit more funds before you are allowed to exit the station. You can find machines for this purpose before you exit through the turnstile.

Purchasing Tickets at Subway Stations

When purchasing tickets at subway stations, machines dispense single-use transportation cards which require a ₩500 deposit. This deposit is refunded at your destination when you return the card to a machine. Look for the deposit refund machine to receive your refund.

1회용 교통카드 [il-hoe-yong gyo-tong-ka-deu] = single use transportation card
보증금 [bo-jeung-geum] = deposit money
보증금 환급기 [bo-jeung-geum hwan-geup-kki] = deposit refund device

Talking on the Subway (Volume)

When people talk on the subway, there is sometimes a noticeable difference in volume between the domestic population and foreigners (particularly from non-Asian countries). Take notice of the volume of chatter around you and try to match that volume, otherwise you may draw some attention. In general, people are not exceptionally quiet on Korean subways, but people will try not to be too noisy as it can be considered to be rude and there is no reason for the whole subway car to know your business.

Changing Sides

Sometimes you will get on the wrong side of the tracks and you'll have to cross over to get to the correct side. When this happens, do not jump the tracks or put your card on the sensor to go out through the turnstile again. Exiting to cross to the other side will charge you for another ride. Instead, head over to the wheelchair access gate and press the button to alert a station worker. Most of the time they will simply press a button to open the gate for you (notified by a short musical jingle). You can then head to the wheelchair access gate on the other side, which is often left waiting unlocked for you by the station staff (if it is not, you can press the button again).

TAXI

여기로 가 주세요. [yeo-gi-ro ga ju-seo-yo.] : **Please go here.**

The phrase literally means "please go here", and if you travel with a map or an address at hand, you can indicate your destination more precisely with the address or by pointing on a map.

This is, of course, the most basic of phrases. If you know your destination or a landmark near your destination (landmarks include large hotels, shopping malls, train stations, department stores, large hospitals, etc.), you can replace 여기 [yeo-gi] with a landmark or area to be more specific about your destination.

After saying the name of the place you want to go to, normally you need to use the location-marking particle **–로** or **–으로**. Even if you don't use it and just say "**인사동 가 주 세요**" [in-sa-dong ga ju-se-yo] instead of "**인사동으로 가 주세요**" [in-sa-dong-eu-ro ga-ju-se-yo], it is perfectly okay and the driver will still understand you.

Sample Sentences

하얏트 호텔로 가 주세요. [ha-yat-teu ho-tel-lo ga ju-se-yo.] = Please go to Hyatt Hotel.

인사동으로 가 주세요. [in-sa-dong-eu-ro ga ju-se-yo.] = Please go to Insadong.

코엑스 가 주세요. [ko-ek-sseu ga ju-se-yo.] = Please go to COEX.

삼성역 가 주세요. [sam-seong-yeok ga ju-se-yo.] = Please go to Samsung Station.

여기 세워 주세요. [yeo-gi se-wo ju-se-yo.] : **Please stand here. / Please drop me off here.**

If you've arrived at your destination, you can tell the driver to let you off with this phrase and the driver will stop and let you off. If you're nearing your destination, you can replace the first word, **여기** [yeo-gi], with (noun + **에서** [e-seo]). 에서 [e-seo] is another location-marking particle which means "at".

The following are words to use when indicating where you want the driver to drop you off. Note that each noun is followed by the Korean word for "at".

- 저 앞 + 에서 = **저 앞에서** [jeo a-pe-seo] = over there up front

- 횡단보도 + 에서 = **횡단보도에서** [hoeong-dan-bo-do-e-seo] = at the crosswalk

- 신호 + 에서 = **신호에서** [si-no-e-seo] = at the traffic light

- 이번 신호 + 에서 = **이번 신호에서** [i-beon si-no-e-seo] = at this traffic light

- 다음 신호 + 에서 = **다음 신호에서** [da-eum si-no-e-seo] = at the next traffic light

- 사거리 + 에서 = **사거리에서** [sa-geo-ri-e-seo] = at the intersection

If you say "**사거리에서 세워 주세요** [sa-geo-ri-e-seo se-wo ju-se-yo]" to ask the driver to drop you off at an intersection, the driver might reply using the expression "**건너서** [geon-neo-seo]", which means "after crossing". If the driver asks "**건너서 세워요?** [geon-neo-seo se-wo-yo?]" (stop after crossing the intersection?) or "**사거리 건너기 전에 세워요?** [sa-geo-ri geon-neo-gi jeo-ne se-wo-yo?]" (stop before crossing the intersection?), you can answer by saying, "**여기 세워 주세요** [yeo-gi se-wo ju-se-yo]" (please drop me off here) or "**건너서 세워 주세요** [geon-neo-seo se-wo ju-se-yo]" (please drop me off after crossing the intersection).

Sample Sentences

횡단보도에서 세워 주세요. [hoeng-dan-bo-do-e-seo se-wo ju-se-yo.] = Please drop me off at the crosswalk.

역에서 세워 주세요. [yeo-ge-seo se-wo ju-se-yo.] = Please drop me off at the station.

저 앞 코너에서 세워 주세요. [jeo ap ko-neo-e-seo se-wo ju-se-yo.] = Please drop me off at the corner over there.

빨리 가 주세요. [ppal-li ga ju-se-yo] : Please go quickly.

Most taxi drivers will make an effort to drive faster and find faster routes if you ask.

네비 찍고 갈 수 있나요? [ne-bi jjik-kko gal ssu in-na-yo?] : May we input the address and go using GPS?

네비 [ne-bi] is derived from **네비게이션** [ne-bi-ge-i-syeon], which simply refers to "navigation" or GPS. **찍다** [jjik-tta] is "to click" or "to type in", in this case. By using "**네비 찍고 갈 수 있나요?**", you are asking if the driver can use the GPS to find the perfect route to reach your destination. Even if you don't say the full phrase very fluently, the moment you say **네비** [ne-bi], most taxi drivers will understand what you mean and check the name of the place or the address with you to be sure before putting it in.

주소 있어요. [ju-so i-sseo-yo.] : I have an address.

No one in Korea knows exact street addresses by heart unless you are going to a big landmark or a place near one. Fortunately, all taxi drivers have GPS to enter in addresses.

카드로 해 주세요. [ka-deu-ro hae ju-se-yo.] : Please charge my card.

교통카드로 할게요. [gyo-tong-ka-deu-ro hal-kke-yo.] : I will pay with a transportation card.

All taxis are equipped with two card readers: a standard credit card reader and a transportation card reader. A transportation card (such as the T-money card) only works on the transportation card reader, but credit cards with a transportation card function can be read on either of the devices.

기사님 [gi-san-nim] : driver

This is the word used to address the driver. You can also use **아저씨** [a-jeo-ssi] (for male driver) or **아주머니** [a-ju-meo-ni] (for female driver), which are broad terms, but most drivers will appreciate being called **기사님**. **기사님** is a more professional term and it has some nuance of respect, more so than **아저씨** or **아주머니**.

거스름돈 [geo-seu-reum-tton] : change

You may hear the driver say "**거스름돈이요** [geo-seu-reum-tto-ni-yo]" when handing you your change. If your driver forgets to give you your change, ask for it by saying "**거스름돈 주세요** [geo-seu-reum-tton ju-se-yo]". If you don't need your change from the driver, you can say "**거스름돈 안 주셔도 돼요** [geo-seu-reum-tton an ju-syeo-do dwae-yo]" or "**거스름돈 괜찮습니다** [geo-seu-reum-tton gwaen-chan-seum-ni-da]", meaning "please keep the change".

안 막히는 데로 가 주세요. [an ma-ki-neun de-ro ga ju-se-yo.] : Please use a route with no traffic.

You may request specific routes to drivers, such as ones with the least amount of traffic. This can also be an easy answer to give when you are asked by the driver which route you want to take.

제일 빠른 데로 가 주세요. [je-il ppa-reun de-ro ga ju-se-yo.] : Please use the fastest route.

고속도로로 가 주세요. [go-sok-tto-ro-ro ga ju-se-yo.] : Please use the expressway.

To give step-by-step directions, use these phrases:

좌회전 해 주세요. [jwa-hoe-jeon hae ju-se-yo.] : **Please turn left.**

우회전 해 주세요. [u-hoe-jeon hae ju-se-yo.] : **Please turn right.**

직진 해 주세요. [jik-jjin hae ju-se-yo.] : **Please go straight.**

유턴 해 주세요. [yu-teon hae ju-se-yo.] : **Please make a U-turn.**

들어가 주세요. [deu-reo-ga ju-se-yo.] : **Please go in.**

To be more specific, you can modify the front of these phrases using the structure "noun + 에서 [e-seo]".

여기에서 좌회전 해 주세요. [yeo-gi-e-seo jwa-hoe-jeon hae ju-se-yo.] : **Please turn left here.**

신호등에서 우회전 해 주세요. [si-no-deung-e-seo u-hoe-jeon hae ju-se-yo.] : **Please turn right at the traffic light.**

은행에서 유턴 해 주세요. [eun-haeng-e-seo yu-teon hae ju-se-yo.] : **Please make a U-turn at the bank.**

이쪽으로 들어가 주세요. [i-jjo-geu-ro deu-reo-ga ju-se-yo.] : **Please go in here.**

Use this to provide turn-by-turn directions to your destination.

미터기 [mi-teo-gi] : meter machine

If the taxi driver suggests a pre-arranged price (usually at a higher price), you may remind the driver to go by meter. This situation usually occurs late at night or when traveling farther distances since drivers are afraid that they will, more than likely, have to come back to the original location without a passenger.

If the driver refuses to turn on the meter, you may get out and wait for a taxi that will use the meter. If you are in Seoul and would like to report the driver, you may use a government hotline by dialing 120. Although refusing to charge by meter is illegal, the public is still very lenient. Almost all taxis will charge by meter within the same city. If you are going to a neighboring city or a distance that is quite far, you will almost always be offered a flat fee. For example, taking a taxi from Seoul to Suwon or from Incheon International Airport to Seoul will often result in a flat rate.

기본 요금 [gi-bon yo-geum] : base fare

The base fare for Seoul taxis as of April 2014 is ₩3,000. Different cities can have different base fares, either slightly cheaper or more expensive.

할증 [hal-jjeung] : extra charge, surcharge

Taxis have a 20% surcharge between the hours of midnight and 4 A.M.

영수증 [yeong-su-jeung] : receipt

All taxis are equipped with a device to print out your receipt whether you pay in cash or with a card. To ask for your receipt, add 주세요 [ju-se-yo], meaning "please give me", to this phrase and say "영수증 주세요 [yeong-su-jeung ju-se-yo]".

골목 [gol-mok] : small road; alley

This term is used to differentiate small roads or alleys from big roads (**큰 길** [keun gil]) when giving directions.

신호 [si-no] / 신호등 [si-no-deung] : traffic light

Use this term as a guide for taxi drivers.

Sample Sentences

저 앞 신호등에서 좌회전해 주세요. [jeo ap si-no-deung-e-seo jwa-hoe-jeon-hae ju-se-yo.] = Turn left at the traffic light over there.

이번 신호에서 유턴해 주세요. [i-beon si-no-e-seo yu-teon-hae ju-se-yo.] = Please make a U-turn at this traffic light.

BREAK TIME

Why No One Knows Addresses

In the past, the Korean government assigned addresses for buildings based on the age and construction date. As a result, there are usually no recognizable patterns to addresses, even for buildings adjacent to each other, which is why no one knows street addresses in Korea. Instead, people rely on major landmarks to give directions, which can include subway stations, major hospitals, universities, large corporate buildings, and intersections. Whether you're living in Korea or traveling, take note of the major landmarks in your area to better assist your driver to getting to the general area of where you want to go. From there, you may be able to give specific directions on which roads to take and where to turn.

The system has changed recently to be more intuitive and easier to remember. It is still in the beginning stages of adoption, and as of early 2014, it has yet to take hold in Korea. As a result, many businesses have to work with two addresses now, and people living in Korea have to know two different street addresses for their home address.

Late Night Taxis

Korea is a very night-centric country with many popular downtown areas. Public transportation is not available 24 hours, and taxis are often the only mode of transportation when subways and buses stop running. On most weekend nights, especially around the time that subway stops running (generally between midnight and 1:30 a.m.), it may be difficult to catch a taxi. Some taxi drivers are very selective and will ask where you are going before they let you in. If you're not going far enough (since "distance = business" for cab drivers), they may say "no" and you will have to find another taxi.

Be sure to check the license plate of a taxi before you get in. Some taxis from other provinces show up late at night, so if you are in Seoul and the cab has a license plate with the word 경기 [gyeong-gi] (referring to Gyeong-gi Province), chances are the driver isn't going to want to take you anywhere in Seoul.

Also, taxis have a 20% surcharge between the hours of midnight and 4 a.m. The base fare starts 20% higher and the meter tends to add up faster.

Types of Taxis

There are several types of taxis, each with slight differences. There are regular taxis, which are often silver, orange, or white. These are basic taxis without any special services. Black taxis (**모범 택시** [mo-beom taek-ssi]) are considered luxury taxis and have more spacious interiors with drivers who are usually more professional and courteous than the average driver. There are also call taxis (**콜 택시** [kol taek-ssi]), which are called over to pick up customers and have an extra surcharge in most cities, usually ₩1,000, if the total fare is not over ₩10,000. People use call taxis in areas where taxis cannot be easily flagged down, when there is a lot of luggage, or if there are too many people and not enough taxis.

Tips:

1. You can use Korea's tourism hotline, 1330 (02-1330 if you are calling from outside of Seoul or with a mobile phone), for help with calling taxis.

2. If you ever feel that a taxi driver has been unfair (i.e. going round about ways, stopping at every stop light, refusing to run the meter), you can call 120 (02-120 if you are calling with a mobile phone) to report the driver. It may also be possible to claim a cash compensation for your troubles.

Taxi Drivers Prefer Cash

All taxis are equipped with card readers and are wirelessly connected to the payment system. As soon as you arrive at your destination and the driver presses the "arrival" button on the machine, the announcement says "please pay by card". Drivers generally prefer cash because they have a fixed amount of money they have to give to their company at the end of each work day, regardless of how much they made on a particular day. Every time a passenger pays with a card, the card payment commission is deducted from their final income. If you travel a long distance and pay much more than the basic fare, most drivers won't mind as much, but if you go a very short distance and try to pay the basic fare of ₩3,000 with a card, the driver might not like it and ask you if you have any cash on you. Most taxi drivers will accept your offer to not receive change; however, if you try to do this or give someone a tip anywhere else (in a restaurant or store, for example), you will surprise and confuse the person to whom you are trying to give the money.

ASKING AND GIVING DIRECTIONS

(place+에) 어떻게 가요? [(place+에) eo-tteo-ke ga-yo?] : How do I get to (place)?

Adjust this phrase by placing the name of the place you're looking for at the beginning of the sentence. If you attach —에 [e] (location particle) to the end of the name of the place, it will be easier for people to understand, but if you forget, it's no big deal. This phrase can be used for both walking directions as well as public transportation.

Sample Sentences

경복궁(에) 어떻게 가요? [gyeong-bok-kkung(-e) eo-tteo-ke ga-yo?] = How do I get to Gyeongbok Palace?

서울역(에) 어떻게 가요? [seo-ul-lyeo-g(e) eo-tteo-ke ga-yo?] = How do I get to Seoul Station?

이태원(에) 어떻게 가요? [i-tae-wo-n(e) eo-tteo-ke ga-yo?] = How do I get to Itaewon?

Here are some common phrases you might hear:

···에서···타세요. [...e-seo ...ta-se-yo.] : Please take the bus/ subway at (place/station).

타세요 [ta-se-yo] means "please ride", and the verb 타다 [ta-da] (to ride) can be used for any vehicle (bus, subway, train, taxi, etc.)

Sample Sentences

건너편에서 143번 버스 타세요. [geon-neo-pyeo-ne-seo baek-sa-sip-ssam-beon beo-sseu ta-se-yo.] = Take bus #143 across the street.

합정역에서 2호선 타세요. [hap-jeong-yeo-ge-seo i-ho-seon ta-se-yo.] = Take Line #2 at Hapjeong Station.

여기에서 아무 버스나 타세요. [yeo-gi-e-seo a-mu beo-sseu-na ta-se-yo.] = Take any bus from here.

···에서 갈아타세요. [...e-seo ga-ra-ta-se-yo.] : Please transfer at (place/station).

갈아타세요 [ga-ra-ta-se-yo] means "please transfer".

Sample Sentences

강남역에서 갈아타세요. [gang-nam-yeo-ge-seo ga-ra-ta-se-yo.] = Transfer at Gangnam Station.

을지병원에서 갈아타세요. [eul-jji-byeong-wo-ne-seo ga-ra-ta-se-yo.] = Transfer at Eulji Hospital.

내려가서 갈아타세요. [nae-ryeo-ga-seo ga-ra-ta-se-yo.] = Go down and transfer.

···에서 내리세요. [...e-seo nae-ri-se-yo.] : Please get off at (place/ station).

내리세요 [nae-ri-se-yo] means "please get off".

Sample Sentences

다음 정류장에서 내리세요. [da-eum jeong-ryu-jang-e-seo nae-ri-se-yo.] = Please get off at the next stop.

명동역에서 내리세요. [myeong-dong-yeo-ge-seo nae-ri-se-yo.] = Please get off at Myeong-dong Station.

세 정거장 뒤에 내리세요. [se jeong-geo-jang dwi-e nae-ri-se-yo.] = Please get off after three stops.

여기 (식당/병원/카페/etc.) + 있어요? [yeo-gi (restaurant/hospital/cafe/etc.) + i-sseo-yo?] : Are there any (restaurants/hospitals/cafes/etc.) around here?

When you are just looking for a specific type of service or place rather than a specific location, you can use this phrase. If you are looking for an inexpensive place to stay for the night, this phrase may be useful when looking for a 찜질방 [jjim-jil-bang] (dry sauna with sleeping areas), which is the most affordable option when looking for a place to sleep.

Sample Sentences

여기 우체국 있어요? [yeo-gi u-che-guk i-sseo-yo?] = Is there a post office around here?

여기 편의점 있어요? [yeo-gi pyeo-nui-jeom i-sseo-yo?] = Is there a convenience store near here?

여기 병원 있어요? [yeo-gi byeong-won i-sseo-yo?] = Is there a hospital around here?

길을 잃었어요. [gi-reul i-reo-sseo-yo.] : I'm lost.

Literally this phrase means "I've lost the road" but is understood as "I'm lost".

제 호텔은/호스텔은 (place) + -에 있어요. [je ho-te-reun/ho-seu-te-reun (place) + e i-sseo-yo.] : My hotel/hostel is at + (place).

Many people may not know the location of your hotel if it is not a major hotel, so be sure to make note of any major landmarks close to your hotel which will make giving/receiving directions easier. Landmarks may include major intersections, banks, subway stations, supermarkets, etc.

오른쪽으로/왼쪽으로 꺾으세요. [o-reun-jjo-geu-ro/oen-jjo-geu-ro kkeo-kkeu-se-yo.] : Turn right/left.

For walking directions, people will say "꺾으세요" or "가세요" [ga-se-yo] more often to mean "to turn", but if you are in a car, you may also hear "우회전/좌회전 하세요" [u-hoe-jeon/jwa-hoe-jeon ha-se-yo] (please turn right/left).

Sample Sentences

여기서 오른쪽으로 꺾으세요. [yeo-gi-seo o-reun-jjo-geu-ro kkeo-kkeu-se-yo.] = Turn right here.

병원 앞에서 왼쪽으로 꺾으세요. [byeong-wo na-pe-seo oen-jjo-geu-ro kkeo-kkeu-se-yo.] = Turn left in front of the hospital.

스타벅스가 보이면 오른쪽으로 꺾으세요. [seu-ta-beok-seu-ga bo-i-myeon o-reun-jjo-geu-ro kkeo-kkeu-se-yo.] = Turn right when you see the Starbucks.

쪽 가세요. [jjuk ga-se-yo] : Go straight.

Another way to say this is "**직진 하세요**" [jik-jjin ha-se-yo], which also means "go straight", but is more often used when in a car.

Sample Sentences

지하철역에서 나와서 **쭉 가세요**. [ji-ha-cheol-lyeo-ge-seo na-wa-seo jjuk ga-se-yo.] = Go out of the subway station and go straight ahead.

그냥 **쭉 가세요**. [geu-nyang jjuk ga-se-yo.] = Go straight.

여기서 이쪽으로 **쭉 가세요**. [yeo-gi-seo i-jjo-geu-reo jjuk ga-se-yo.] = Keep going straight ahead from here.

사거리 [sa-geo-ri] : intersection

Most people don't know the names of streets, but many do know the names of major intersections. Intersections are an integral part of receiving/giving directions in Korea and are often used as reference points. Many intersections have specific names which are commonly influenced by a nearby landmark.

건너편 [geon-neo-pyeon] : across the street

Another form of this word is **맞은편** [ma-jeun-pyeon], which means "the opposite side". Both terms are used frequently.

건너세요. [geon-neo-se-yo.] = Please cross (place).

건너세요 is used often when giving/receiving directions.

Sample Sentences

횡단보도를 **건너세요.** [hoeng-dan-bo-do-reul geon-neo-se-yo.] = Cross the street at the crosswalk.
길을 **건너세요.** [gi-reul geon-neo-se-yo.] = Cross the street.
강을 **건너세요.** [gang-eul geon-neo-se-yo.] = Cross the river.

여기로/저기로 [yeo-gi-ro/jeo-gi-ro] : (to) here, this way/(to) there, that way

This phrase can be used when guiding someone by pointing in a specific direction or even when pointing to a place on a map.

Sample Sentences

(Looking at a map) **여기로** 가면 은행이 보일 거예요. [yeo-gi-ro ga-myeon eun-haeng-i bo-il kkeo-ye-yo]. = If you go here/this way, you will see a bank (pointing in a direction).
저기로 가서 길을 건너시면 돼요. [jeo-gi-ro ga-seo gi-reul geon-neo-si-myeon dwae-yo.] = Go that way and cross the street.

(building/place) + 이/가 보일 거예요. [(building/place) + i/ga bo-il kkeo-ye-yo.] : You will see ...

This phrase is essential since giving directions in Korea is largely based on memorable landmarks. Many people will refer to banks, coffee shops, stores, etc. to describe which direction to go instead of street names.

지하도 [ji-ha-do] : underpass (pedestrian)

Underpasses in Korea are not only paths to get on the other side of the street without having to deal with street traffic; they are also often connected to underground shopping malls. The stores in these underpasses are usually cheaper than those found above ground.

(name of a station) + -역에서 (지하철을) 타서 + (name of a station) + -역에서 내리세요. [(name of a station) + yeo-ge-seo (ji-ha-cheo-reul) ta-seo (name of a station) + yeo-ge-seo nae-ri-se-yo] : Take the subway at (name of a station) + station and get off at (name of a station) + station.

If you know which subway station you need to leave from and which one you will be arriving at, you can use one of the numerous Seoul subway applications on your cell phone (with English menus) which will calculate the best routes from one station to another.

Sample Sentences

압구정역에서 타서 을지로3가역에서 내리세요. [ap-kku-jeong-yeo-ge-seo ta-seo eul-jji-ro-sam-ga-yeo-ge-seo nae-ri-se-yo.] = Take the subway at Apgujeong Station and get off at Euljiro-3-ga Station.

명동역에서 타서 사당역에서 내리세요. [myeong-dong-yeo-ge-seo ta-seo sa-dang-yeo-ge-seo nae-ri-se-yo.] = Take the subway at Myeongdong Station and get off at Sadang Station.

(number) + -번 버스 타서 + (name of a bus stop) + -에서 내리세요. [(number) + beon beo-sseu ta-seo (name of a bus stop) + e-seo nae-ri-se-yo.] : Take bus + (number) and get off at + (name of bus stop).

After receiving these instructions and taking the bus, you may want to listen carefully to the bus announcements since Korean may be the only language which is used. There are occasional English, Japanese, and Chinese announcements, but those are typically reserve for major stops only. Even if you are approaching a major stop, you may not hear an announcement in a language other than Korean.

Sample Sentences

302번 버스 타서 경복궁에서 내리세요. [sam-bae-gi-beon beo-sseu ta-seo kyeong-bok-kkung-e-seo nae-ri-se-yo.] = Take bus 302 and get off at Gyeongbokgung.

9100번 버스 타서 서현역에서 내리세요. [gu-il-gong-gong-beon beo-sseu ta-seo seo-hyeon-yeo-ge-seo nae-ri-se-yo.] = Take Bus 9100 and get off at Seohyeon Station.

*Tip: The way bus numbers are said is a personal preference and will differ from person to person. Some people prefer to say the whole number, including the words for "thousand" and "hundred" (see first example above), while others say each number individually (see second example above).

골목 [gol-mok] : alley

You can find many small alleys in Korea called 골목. When something is not near a big road, but rather up a small alley, you will hear people explaining how to get there using this word, such as in 이 골목 [i gol-mok], 저 골목 [jeo gol-mok], 첫번째 골목 [cheot-ppeon-jjae gol-mok] or 두 번째 골목 [du-beon-jjae gol-mok].

Sample Dialogue

A: 인사동에 어떻게 가요? [in-sa-dong-e eo-tteo-ke ga-yo?] = How do I get to Insadong?
B: 저기 사거리에서 오른쪽으로 꺾으세요. [jeo-gi sa-geo-ri-e-seo o-reun-jjo-geu-ro kkeo-kkeu-se-yo.] = Turn right at the intersection there.

A: 여기 편의점 있어요? [yeo-gi pyeo-nui-jeom i-sseo-yo?] = Is there a convenience store here?
B: 횡단보도 건너서 쭉 가세요. [hoeng-dan-bo-do geon-neo-seo jjuk ga-se-yo.] = Go straight after you cross the street at the crosswalk.

BREAK TIME

Smartphone Applications for Directions

There are several subway applications for smart phones that calculate the best routes and have timetables, travel time, price, and some even have English menus. Bus applications, in addition to providing standard route information, travel time, and other basic information, are connected to GPS systems. These applications can show the accurate location of each bus on the route and arrival times. Bus applications do require rudimentary Korean typing ability as most bus stops are in Korean and do not have an English spelling.

Tourist Help

In Seoul, places like Insadong, Myeongdong, Hongdae, Ehwa University, Itaewon, etc. have government-hired tourist guides, called 관광 통역 안내원 [gwan-gwang tong-yeok an-nae-won], who help tourists find places and give recommendations. They can often be found on the busiest corners of the area, usually standing in pairs. The guides are easily visible with their red hats, jackets, and shirts, and are multilingual, usually in English, Japanese, and Chinese. Look for these tourist guides if you need help with directions or would like to get a recommendation on food or things to do in the area.

SHOP-PING

FASHION

입어 보다 [i-beo-bo-da] : to try (something) on

Some independent stores won't allow female customers to try on clothes since makeup can easily be transferred onto clothes. This is especially true for smaller stores and stores in markets such as Dongdaemun.

Sample Sentences

이거 입어 봐도 돼요? [i-geo i-beo bwa-do dwae-yo?] = Can I try this on?

어디서 입어 볼 수 있어요? [eo-di-seo i-beo bol ssu i-sseo-yo?] = Where can I try this on?

한번 입어 볼게요. [han-beon i-beo bol-kke-yo.] = I will try this on.

교환 [gyo-hwan] : exchange
환불 [hwan-bul] : refund, return

While major retailers and global brands will allow refunds and exchanges without question, some independent shops will not allow any refunds, even with a receipt. This is

typical for smaller, cheaper shops that are privately owned. These shops sometimes will allow exchanges, but be aware that at many small shops, sales are final.

Sample Sentences

교환 돼요? [gyo-hwan dwae-yo?] = Are exchanges okay?
교환해 주세요. [gyo-hwa-nae ju-se-yo.] = Please exchange this for me.
교환은 안 돼요. [gyo-hwa-neun an dwae-yo.] = We don't do exchanges.

환불해 주세요. [hwan-bu-rae ju-se-yo.] = Please give me a refund.
환불은 안 돼요. [hwan-bu-reun an dwae-yo.] = We don't do returns.

피팅룸 있어요? [pi-ting-ru mi-sseo-yo?] : Is there a fitting room?
피팅룸 어디 있어요? [pi-ting-ru meo-di-i-sseo-yo?] : Where is the fitting room?

"Fitting room" is the same word in Korean, but the Korean pronunciation is different since there is no "F" sound in Korean. This word is said with a "P" sound (ㅍ) and should be pronounced accordingly in order to be better understood.

교환, 환불은 7일 이내로 택 떼지 마시고 영수증 지참하셔서 가져오셔야 돼요. [gyo-hwan, hwan-bu-reun chi-ri ri-nae-ro taek tte-ji ma-si-go yeong-su-jeung ji-cham-ha-syeo-seo ga-jyeo-o-syeo-ya dwae-yo.] : In order to receive a refund or do an exchange, please bring back the item within 7 days with the receipt and without removing the tag.

This is a common phrase, especially at higher end shopping establishments like department stores. It is also used at retail shopping malls. However, sometimes this phrase is not heard at all and sales are final.

택 [taek] : tag

Price tags are common in retail shops and department stores, but for many smaller shops, clothes may not have tags. This is also related to refund/exchange policies.

Sample Sentences

택 제거하시면 환불 안 돼요. [taek je-geo-ha-si-myeon hwan-bul an dwae-yo.] = If you remove the price tag, you can't return it.

택에 써 있는 가격에서 10% 할인해 드려요. [tae-ge sseo in-neun ga-gyeo-ge-seo sip-peu-ro ha-rin-hae deu-ryeo-yo.] = We give you a 10% discount from the price written on the tag.

사이즈 하나 더 큰/작은 거 있어요? [sa-i-jeu ha-na deo keun/ja-geun geo i-sseo-yo?] : Do you have one size bigger/smaller?

Most global retail stores will have sizes up to Extra Large (XL). However, for domestic Korean clothing, larger sizes are often difficult to come by.

More Words

티셔츠/티 [ti-syeo-cheu]/[ti]	t-shirt
치마 [chi-ma]	skirt
바지 [ba-ji]	pants
청바지 [cheong-ba-ji]	jeans
스웨터 [seu-we-teo]	sweater
후드티 [hu-deu-ti]	hoodie
남방 [nam-bang]	casual shirt
자켓 [ja-ket]	jacket
잠바 [jam-ba]	jacket (**잠바** comes from "jumper")
코트 [ko-teu]	coat
신발 [sin-bal]	shoes
구두 [gu-du]	dress shoes
운동화 [un-dong-hwa]	sneakers, running shoes, tennis shoes
양말 [yang-mal]	socks
장갑 [jang-gap]	gloves
목걸이 [mok-kkeo-ri]	necklace
귀걸이 [gwi-geo-ri] / **귀고리** [gwi-go-ri]	earrings
팔찌 [pal-jji]	bracelet
수영복 [su-yeong-bok]	swimsuit
속옷 [so-got]	underwear
와이셔츠 [wa-i-syeo-cheu]	dress shirt
	* "Y-shirt" is a Koreanized English word that refers to dress shirts with collars and buttons.
원피스 [won-pi-seu]	dress
	* This is an English word used in Korean to refer to a one-piece dress.
스카프 [seu-ka-peu]	scarf

목도리 [mok-tto-ri]

scarf

* **스카프**, the Korean pronunciation of the word "scarf", is for smaller/lighter scarves that can be worn in autumn or spring. **목도리** is for larger/thicker scarves that are usually worn in the winter.

BREAK TIME

Sizes

Korea uses the general sizing scale of small, medium, and large. However, a medium size in Korea may be different from a medium from your own country depending on where you're from (Korean sizes tend to be smaller than those in Western countries). Extra large sizes are often difficult to find in Korea, especially when it comes to domestically made clothes and shoes. Also, for domestically produced fashion, you may come across the domestic Korean metric for sizes, given in centimeters (90, 95, 100, 105, etc.) It isn't as widely used as it once was, but it is still found for domestically produced clothes.

FEMALE CLOTHING SIZE					
International	XS	S	M	L	XL
Korean	44	55	66	77	88
Chest (cm)	81-83	83-89	89-96	96-103	103-107
(inch)	32	33-34	35-37	38-40	42
Waist (cm)	61-63	63-68	68-75	75-81	81-86
(inch)	24	25-26	27-29	30-32	34
Hip (cm)	86-89	89-92	92-99	99-106	106-112
(inch)	34	35-36	37-39	40-42	/ 44

MALE CLOTHING SIZE					
International	XS	S	M	L	XL
Korean	90	95	100	105	110
Chest (cm)	72-86	86-98	98-109	109-115	
(inch)	28-34	35-39	40-43	44-45	
Height (cm)	155-165	165-175	175-185	175-185	
(inch)	61-65	65-69	69-73	69-73	

For larger sizes, you can find larger-sized clothing in the Itaewon area of Seoul.

Dongdaemun - Home of Korean Fashion

If you're looking for uniquely Korean fashion, you should head to Dongdaemun, Seoul. This is THE fashion district of Seoul and is the largest supplier of Korean fashion. Most independent shops and stores in Korea are supplied by the wholesale stores in Dongdaemun, and as a result, some stores will have the same items. To find the most variety and selection, head to Dongdaemun, the source of Korea's fashion industry.

Credit Card vs Cash

Nearly all vendors in Korea accept credit cards. However, cash is more tax-friendly for businesses and, therefore, is the preferred payment by smaller shops. As a result, most smaller shops will add a markup for credit card purchases (usually about 10% above the advertised price to make up for the Value Added Tax). This is technically illegal, but smaller shops tend to do this. Larger retail stores found in shopping malls and big streets will not do this.

GROCERY SHOPPING

(item) + 어디 있어요? [(item) eo-di i-sseo-yo?] : Where is (item)?

Most supermarket layouts in Korea are similar to those in other countries. Produce and meat are on the outer edges with packaged and processed foods towards the center of the store.

봉투 드릴까요? [bong-tu deu-ril-kka-yo?] : Do you need a plastic/paper bag?

종이 봉투 [jong-i bong-tu] = paper bag

종량제 봉투 [jong-ryang-je bong-tu] = registered garbage bag

→ Also known as **쓰레기 봉투** [sseu-re-gi bong-tu] = garbage bag

Larger supermarkets will ask you this question. If you reply with **네** [ne] (yes), you will be charged a small fee for each bag. Most plastic bags that you receive at the checkout stand in large supermarkets are **종량제 봉투** [jong-ryang-je bong-tu], or registered garbage bags. These bags are certified to use for trash pick up. If you use a non-registered bag, your

trash won't be picked up. The word **봉지** [bong-ji] is sometimes used instead of **봉투**. Small shops on the other hand, or shops where the clerk doesn't ask whether you want a plastic bag or not, offer plastic bags for free since these bags cannot be doubled as official trash bags.

포인트 카드 [po-in-teu ka-deu] : point card

Most chain supermarkets have point card systems that act like frequent flyer miles. By buying products from a store often, one can build up points to use toward free items or discounted goods.

행사 상품 [haeng-sa sang-pum] : promotional/discounted product
2+1 [tu-peul-leo-sseu-won] : buy 2, get 1 free

Many promotional events (**행사**) in Korea revolve around the 2+1 model, where with the purchase of two, a third is free. The numbers vary, and you will often see 1+1 or 3+1 deals. Smaller neighborhood supermarkets do offer these promotions, but this type of deal is more often found at larger retailers.

국내산 [gung-nae-san] : domestic product (Korea-produced)

In Korea, it is a law to state where food products originate. Supermarkets and restaurants will have signs indicating the source of the meats or vegetables. The following are common source nations:

미국산 [mi-guk-ssan] = Produced in the United States

호주산 [ho-ju-san] = Produced in Australia

중국산 [jung-guk-ssan] = Produced in China

배달해 주세요. [bae-dal-hae ju-se-yo.] : Please deliver it for me.

Some supermarkets will deliver groceries to your door for free. For most deliveries, there is a minimum purchase amount that must be met in order to take advantage of the service. Use this phrase to indicate that you would like delivery service.

(type of meat) (number) + -근/그램 주세요. [(type of meat) (number) + -geun/geu-raem ju-se-yo.] : Please give me (number) geun/grams of (type of meat).

근 is a Korean quantity word used for meat servings as well as some produce items. For meat, one 근 is equal to approximately 600 grams, a half 근 is 300 grams. Instead of 근, you can also use grams. "Gram" in Korean is 그램, but some people pronounce it as 그람 [geu-ram] as well.

한 근 [han-geun] = 600g

반 근 [ban-geun] = 300g

Sample Sentences

200그램 주세요. [i-baek-kkeu-raem ju-se-yo.] = Please give me 200 grams.
300그람 주세요. [sam-baek-kkeu-ram ju-se-yo.] = Please give me 300 grams.
한 근 반 주세요. [han geun ban ju-se-yo.] = Please give me one and a half geun (900g).

(name of a fish) (number) + - 마리 주세요. [saeng-seon (number) + - ma-ri ju-se-yo.] : Please give (number) of (name of a fish).

마리 is the counter for animals, such as fish and chicken.

손질해 주세요. [son-jil-hae ju-se-yo.] : **Please gut the fish.**

Normally, wherever you buy fish, the store or shop have already scaled, gutted, and cleaned the fish for purchase. However, if the fish is fresh and untouched, you can ask someone to do the dirty work for you by using the phrase.

유통기한 [yu-tong-gi-han] : **expiration date**

제조일로부터 ⋯ [je-jo-il-lo-bu-teo ...]: (a certain number of days/months/years) from the day it was made

Expiration dates are printed on all packaged food products. For some products, however, the date the item was produced is also printed. The date with the word **까지** [kka-ji] (until) next to it is the expiration date.

할부 어떻게 해 드릴까요? [hal-bu eo-tteo-ke hae deu-ril-kka-yo?] : How shall I charge it?

This phrase is heard when a cashier receives a credit card. Korean credit cards work through 할부, the division of one specific payment over several months. If the bill at the supermarket is ₩100,000, you can divide that by two months and pay ₩50,000 the first month and ₩50,000 the next month. This can be done by the cashier. Depending on the card, you can pay off your amount over several months with or without interest. You may respond by saying the number of preferred months (**3개월** [sam-gae-wol], **5개월** [o-gae-wol], etc.), or by politely refusing by saying "**괜찮아요** [gwen-cha-na-yo]" or "**일시불로 해 주세요** [il-ssi-bul-lo hae ju-se-yo]", meaning, "it's okay" or "no installment payments, please".

When ordering meat at a supermarket or a butcher shop, you may want to clarify the type of meat as well as what it's for so the meat can be prepared accordingly.

Type of Meats

고기 [go-gi]	meat
돼지고기 [dwae-ji-go-gi]	pork
소고기 [so-go-gi]	beef
닭고기 [dak-kko-gi]	chicken
스테이크용 [seu-te-i-keu-yong]	for steak
찌개용 [jji-gae-yong]	for Korean stews
구이용 [gu-i-yong]	for grilling
국거리 [guk-kkeo-ri]	for Korean soups
갈아 놓은 고기 [ga-ra no-eun go-gi]	ground meat

Sample Sentences

구이용 돼지고기 1근 주세요. [gu-i-yong dwe-ji-go-gi han-geun ju-se-yo.] = Please give me one geun of pork for grilling.

찌개용 닭고기 100그램 주세요. [jji-gae-yong dalk-kko-gi baek-geu-ram ju-se-yo.] = Please give me 100 grams of chicken for (use in) stew.

Here are some name of fish/seafood:

Name of Fish/Seafood

생선 [saeng-seon]	fish
고등어 [go-deung-eo]	mackerel
농어 [nong-eo]	sea bass
갈치 [gal-chi]	cutlassfish
송어 [song-eo]	trout
참치 [cham-chi]	tuna
연어 [yeo-neo]	salmon
장어 [jang-eo]	eel
오징어 [o-jing-eo]	squid
새우 [sae-u]	shrimp
조개 [jo-gae]	clam
홍합 [hong-hap]	mussel

Here are some other nouns you might need that are related to grocery shopping:

More Words

두부 [du-bu]	tofu

씨리얼 [ssi-ri-eol]	cereal
라면 [ra-myeon]	ramen noodles
과자 [gwa-ja]	snacks
과일 [gwa-il]	fruit
채소 [chae-so]	vegetable
유제품 [yu-je-pum]	dairy
냉동 식품 [naeng-dong sik-pum]	frozen food
우유 [u-yu]	milk
술 [sul]	alcohol
비누 [bi-nu]	soap
치약 [chi-yak]	toothpaste
칫솔 [chit-ssol]	toothbrush
휴지 [hyu-ji]	toilet paper; tissue

Sample Dialogue

Cashier: **봉투 드릴까요?** [bong-tu deu-ril-kka-yo?] = Do you need a plastic/paper bag?

Customer: **네.** [ne.]/**아니요.** [a-ni-yo.] = Yes./No.

Cashier: (If the customer says yes) **종이 봉투로 드릴까요, 종량제 봉투로 드릴까요?** [jong-i-bong-tu-ro deu-ril-kka-yo, jong-ryang-je bong-tu-ro deu-ril-kka-yo?] = Do you want a paper bag or a garbage bag?

Customer: **종이 봉투로 주세요.** [jong-i bong-tu-ro ju-se-yo.]/**종량제 봉투로 주세요.** [jong-ryan-je bong-tu-ro ju-se-yo.] = Paper bag, please./Garbage bag, please.

Cashier: **포인트 카드 가지고 계신가요?** [po-in-teu ka-deu ga-ji-go gye-sin-ga-yo?] = Do you have a point card?

Customer: **네.** [ne.]/**아니요.** [a-ni-yo.]

Cashier: (If the customer pays with a credit card) **할부 어떻게 해 드릴까요?** [hal-bu eo-tteo-ke hae deu-ril-kka-yo?] = How shall I charge it?

Customer: **일시불로 해 주세요.** [il-ssi-bul-lo hae ju-se-yo.]/**3개월로 해 주세요.** [sam-gae-wol-lo hae ju-se-yo.] = Just a single payment, please./ Three-month installment plan please.

BREAK TIME

Using a coin to use a shopping cart

If you need a shopping cart, you'll need a ₩100 coin. Supermarket carts are lined up and locked together with a coin-operated mechanism. Insert a ₩100 coin and the cart will unlock. Remove the lock from the cart in front and you're free to move around with the sidewinding, fast and furious, drifting Korean grocery carts. To get your ₩100 back, return the cart to any cart corral and insert the lock into the cart in front, and your coin should pop out of the lock. It's a simple way for shoppers to bring back shopping carts to the proper place.

Snacking on Samples

Korean supermarkets often have free food samples to try. Workers will stand near promotional products and cook/prepare the product on the spot. Any customer can go to a sampling stand to try the food. The servings are small, and customers often take more than one sample, but taking too much is frowned upon. To find the most variety of samples, go to supermarkets in the evening or on weekends.

Foreign Food Products

Most Korean supermarkets carry basic non-Korean food products, such as pasta, bread, cereal, and other foods that have made their way into the average Korean diet. Anything more than basic products or foods must be imported and are often not sold in the average supermarket. Imported food products can be found at foreign supermarkets, department stores that sell food, or supermarkets in neighborhoods with a large population of foreign visitors or residents.

INTERNET SHOPPING

While you are in Korea, you might have to or want to sign up for certain services on the Internet, especially when you buy things online. Although more and more websites offer English menus and global services, learning some basic Internet-related words and phrases will come in handy.

COMMON WEBSITE WORDS AND PHRASES

These are some of the most frequently used words you will encounter on almost every Korean website that requires signing up and signing in:

Common Website Words and Phrases

아이디 [a-i-di]	ID
비밀번호 [bi-mil-beon-ho]	password (literal meaning: "secret number")
패스워드 [pae-sseu-wo-deu]	password
아이디·비밀번호 찾기 [ai-i-di bi-mil-beon-ho chat-kki]	Forgot ID/PW?
로그인 [lo-geu-in]	log in
로그아웃 [lo-geu-a-ut]	log out
로그인 상태 유지 [lo-geu-in sang-tae yu-ji]	stay logged in
검색 [geom-saek]	search
즐겨찾기 [jeul-gyeo-chat-kki]	bookmark / favorites

WEBSITE REGISTRATION

Many Korean online shops are limited to registered members and require user registration for further access. When registering to become a member, most of the time there is no English version of the registration page. Instead of just randomly clicking around and guessing what something means during the sign-up process, refer to the list below!

회원가입 [hoe-won-ga-ip] / 가입하기 [ga-i-pa-gi]: sign-up/registration

The website registration process starts by clicking on the word **회원가입** or **가입하기**. The word **회원** means "membership" and **가입** means "registration".

성명 [seong-myeong]: name

성명 is a more formal version of the common Korean word for "name", **이름** [i-reum].

이메일 [i-me-il]: e-mail

연락처 [yeol-lak-cheo]: phone number

Another word for phone number is **전화번호** [jeo-nwa-beo-no].

주민 등록 번호 [ju-min deung-nok beo-no]: Resident Registration Number

Many websites require users to register website IDs by providing a resident registration numbers, a number that all Korean citizens are given. It is similar to national identification numbers in other countries.

외국인 등록 번호 [oe-gu-gin deung-nok beo-no]: Alien Registration Number

This number is given to foreign residents to serve as an identification number when coming to Korea on a certain type of visa, such as a student or working visa. Resident foreigners (depending on the type of visa) can receive an Alien Registration Number (**외국인 등록 번호**) and an Alien Registration Card (**외국인 등록증** [oe-gu-gin deung-nok-jjeung]). Some websites are difficult to sign up for as a foreigner, but this has changed in recent years now that most major websites have extended sign-ups to include foreigners with an Alien Registration Number.

본인 인증 [bo-ni nin-jeung]: identity confirmation

For certain registration signups, identity confirmation is also required. This is typically done by sending a pin number to a mobile phone that was registered using the same resident registration number, **주민 등록 번호** [ju-min deun-nok beo-no], or foreigner registration number, **외국인 등록 번호** [oe-gu-gin deung-nok beo-no].

개인 정보 [gae-in jeong-bo]: personal information

동의 [dong-ui] / 동의 안 함 [dong-ui an ham]: accept / do not accept

For sites with user agreements, there are several terms and conditions documents that the user must accept in order to continue with signing up. These agreements are usually in relation to how personal information can be or is going to be used for website management and future promotions.

개인 회원 [gae-in hoe-won]: personal account

Some websites allow a choice between personal accounts, 개인 회원, and corporate accounts, 법인 회원 [beo-bin hoe-won].

SHOPPING

Once you are finished with the sign-up process, you will need to know these following words to actually order something.

구매하기 [gu-mae-ha-gi]: purchase

바로 구매 [ba-ro gu-mae]: purchase now

Clicking either of these purchase buttons on shopping websites will take you to the checkout page where you can complete your transaction.

비회원 구매 [bi-hoe-won gu-mae]: purchase without login

Some websites will allow purchases without user registration.

위시 리스트 [wi-ssi li-seu-teu]: wish list

The "wish list" is for items that you hope to buy in the future, whereas the shopping cart is for items you wish to purchase immediately or in the very near future.

장바구니 [jang-ba-gu-ni]: shopping cart

Add items to your shopping cart by clicking the button with this word on it, which is quite typical of nearly all shopping websites where you can browse through many items. The shopping cart also saves your items and allows your items to be purchased at a later time.

배송비 [bae-song-bi]: shipping fee

Free shipping is marked as **무료 배송** [mu-ryo bae-song]. Most Korean websites offer free shipping for items or combinations of items that are over a certain amount. Even if you don't reach that certain amount, the basic shipping fee within Korea is quite affordable at ₩2,500 for items of most sizes and weights.

구매 수량 [gu-mae su-ryang]: quantity (of items to be purchased)

Change this number to order as many or as few of the same item as you want.

PAYMENT

Once you have chosen the items you'd like to purchase, you can head over to the "checkout" or "payment" page. Even if you know and understand all of the following words, another possible challenge is going through the security steps and software installations. In the recent past, most online shopping sites only worked with Internet Explorer because of a Korean law that required the installation of Active X plug-ins, but this is slowly changing. As of March 2014, many of the most widely used online shopping malls now allow payments on other types of web browsers and operating systems, including mobile devices.

결제하기 [gyeol-jje-ha-gi]: pay

결제 수단 [gyeol-jje su-dan]: payment method

You can pay for your products using various payment methods, including a credit card.

카드 종류 [ka-deu jong-ryu]: card type

Choose the issuing credit card bank or company.

신용 카드 [si-nyong ka-deu]: credit card

Using a credit card is the most common way to pay online. For many foreigners, it can be difficult to obtain a Korean credit card, but many websites will recognize and accept most internationally recognized credit card brands.

무통장 입금 [mu-tong-jang ip-kkeum]: bank transfer

This allows shoppers without credit cards to pay through bank transfer. You can do a bank transfer for free via a smartphone application or at bank ATMs.

일시불 [il-ssi-bul]: pay in full

할부 [hal-bu]: monthly installments

Credit cards in Korea allow for credit card purchases to be added in full to the next month's credit card bill, known as **일시불**. Another option is to charge your card in equal monthly installments, or **할부**. The credit card holder chooses the amount of months, and the price is then divided evenly among the months. Depending on the credit card company's policies, the first few months of **할부** can be without interest.

핸드폰 소액 결제 [haen-deu-pon so-aek gyeol-jje]: paying with a phone

Some online shopping websites allow you to pay by adding the price onto the next month's phone bill. This is usually available for smaller payments.

DELIVERY

Before your online purchase is complete, if you don't already have an address registered on the website, you will have to enter your address. Knowing the following words will be helpful when entering an address:

받으시는 분 [ba-deu-si-neun bun]: recipient

주소 [ju-so]: address

배송 메시지 [bae-song me-ssi-ji]: delivery message

This text field is used if you have special instructions for the delivery person. Common instructions include:

- 경비실에 맡겨 주세요. [gyeong-bi-si-re mat-kkyeo ju-se-yo.]: Please leave it at the front desk

- 집 앞 편의점에 맡겨 주세요. [ji bap pyeon-nui-jeo-me mat-kkyeo ju-se-yo.]: Please leave it at the convenience store in front of the house.

- 12시전까지 와주세요. [yeol-du-si-jeon-kka-ji wa-ju-se-yo.]: Please come before 12.

BREAK TIME

Search in Korea

The biggest search portals in Korea are Naver.com and Daum.net. Together, these two search portals account for a large majority of Internet searches in Korea. Google does have a growing presence in Korea, but it is still not as popular as Naver (네이버 [ne-i-beo]) or Daum (다음 [da-eum]). After learning some Korean, you will find that using Naver or Daum to be much more convenient while you are in Korea.

Gmarket

Gmarket, which is owned by eBay, is Korea's largest online store and Korea's version of Amazon.com. It sells everything from books and laundry detergent to bottled water and televisions. There is an English version of the website, but the product descriptions are often still in Korean.

Mac vs Windows

Although Apple computers have been gaining popularity in Korea, many computers are equipped with Windows operating systems. Many websites and programs in Korea are reliant on Windows-based security features which often require downloading and installing security programs that cannot work with iOS. These security feature requirements were initially written into a law but have since been repealed.

DAILY LIFE

HAIR
SALON

When you walk into a hair salon, you will be greeted by staff and asked one of (or a variation of) the following questions:

예약하고 오셨어요? [ye-ya-ka-go o-syeo-sseo-yo?] : Did you make a reservation already?

Most hair salons accept reservations and may not take walk-ins. It is not advisable to walk in and try to get an appointment that day since you might have to wait for a long time, especially if it's at a larger salon.

어떤 거 하러 오셨어요? [eo-tteon geo ha-reo o-syeo-sseo-yo?] : How may we help you?

When the hair salon receptionist (or the owner of the hair salon if it is a small salon) doesn't know whether you want to get a haircut, a perm, styling, or a treatment, he/she will ask you this question. 어떤 거 literally means "what kind of thing", so listen for this expression!

뭐 하시게요? [mwo ha-si-ge-yo?] : How may I help you?

The way "how may I help you?" is said to you really depends on the person. In addition to this phrase, another common phrase is "뭐 하시게요?", meaning "what do you intend to do?"

Alternatively, since the majority of people want either a haircut or a perm, hairdressers might ask you these following two questions separately or together:

커트 하시게요? [keo-teu ha-si-ge-yo?] / 커트 하시려고요? [keo-teu

ha-si-ryeo-go-yo?] : **Do you want a haircut?**

파마 하시게요? [pa-ma-ha-si-ge-yo?] / **파마 하시려고요?** [pa-ma ha-si-ryeo-go-yo?] : **You want a perm?**

담당 선생님 있으신가요? [dam-dang seon-saeng-nim i-sseu-sin-ga-yo?] : Do you have a designated hairdresser?

Many chain hair salons have the designated hairdresser system so you can be assured that your hairdresser knows your hair style and preferences as well as your hair's traits. If you are traveling for a short period of time and do not visit a hair salon regularly, you can simply reply to this question by saying, "**아니요**" [a-ni-yo]" to mean "no", and the staff will have any available hairdresser serve you.

The following are some answers you can give to the hair salon staff when you are faced with the questions above:

머리 자르려고요. [meo-ri ja-reu-ryeo-go-yo.] / 커트 하려고요. [keo-teu ha-ryeo-go-yo.] : I want to get a haircut.

머리 means "head" or "hair" and **자르려고요** means "I want to cut", but the English word "cut" is also very commonly used to mean "haircut".

파마 하려고요. [pa-ma ha-ryeo-go-yo.] : I want to get my hair permed.

파마 is the Konglish word for "perm". However, **펌** [peom], the Korean pronunciation for the English word "perm", is also commonly understood nowadays.

매직 하려고요. [mae-jik ha-ryeo-go-yo.] / 스트레이트 하려고요. [seu-teu-re-i-teu ha-ryeo-go-yo.]: I want to get my hair straightened.

매직, the Konglish word for "magic", refers to a type of straightening perm in Korea (and Asia in general) that makes hair straight, thin, smooth, and shiny (the degree differs according to natural hair type). It is a long-term perm that can last up to a year, or at least until the perm grows out. This perm is similar to a Brazilian Blowout or a Keratin Complex.

스트레이트 is a perm that is less intense than 매직. Your hair will look a little more natural with a 스트레이트 than with 매직.

염색 하려고요. [yeom-saek ha-ryeo-go-yo.] : I want to dye my hair.

염색 is the Korean word for "dye". To be specific about what color your would like, you can just say this phrase and point to a color you want in a hairstyle brochure or photo, or you can use the next phrase (see below).

(color) + –색으로 염색해 주세요. [(color) + sae-geu-ro yeom-sae-kae ju-se-yo.] : Please dye my hair (color).

Colors

빨간색 [ppal-gan-saek]	red
검은색 [geo-meun-saek]	black
갈색 [gal-ssaek]	brown
밝은 갈색 [bal-geun gal-ssaek]	bright brown
어두운 갈색 [eo-du-un gal-ssaek]	dark brown
파란색 [pa-ran-saek]	blue
노란색 [no-ran-saek]	yellow

Sample Sentences

검은색으로 염색해 주세요. [geo-meun-sae-geu-ro yeom-sae-kae ju-se-yo.] = Please dye my hair black.

빨간색으로 염색해 주세요. [ppal-gan-sae-geu-ro yeom-sae-kae ju-se-yo.] = Please dye my hair red.

After you have been greeted by the hair salon staff and you have told them what kind of service you want to get, you can use the following phrases to talk more specifically with your hairdresser about what you want.

원하시는 스타일 있나요? [won-ha-si-neun seu-ta-il in-na-yo?] : Is there any particular style you want?

Perms, treatments, and haircuts may not have the same name in Korean as in English (mohican, layered, double cut, etc.) The easiest way to communicate with the stylist is to bring a picture of your desired cut. Another alternative is to tell the stylist how you would like your hair cut by pointing to different parts of your hair and describing what you want.

얼마나 잘라 드릴까요? [eol-ma-na jal-la deu-ril-kka-yo?] : How much should I cut?

The key words to listen for are **얼마나** (how much) and **잘라** (cut). One way to reply is to use the next phrase "**여기까지** [yeo-gi-kka-ji]" (until here).

여기까지 잘라 주세요. [yeo-gi-kka-ji jal-la ju-se-yo.] : Please cut until here.

Use your hands to show the exact length you would like your hair to be cut. The key words are: **여기**, meaning "here", and **까지**, meaning "until".

···cm 정도 잘라 주세요. [(number) sen-chi jeong-do jal-la ju-se-yo.] : Please cut around (number) cm.

You can be specific with the exact length of hair you would like to cut. The Korean pronunciation of "centimeter" is roughly similar to English, **센티미터** [sen-ti-mi-teo]. However, in everyday life, **센티미터** is used as **센치** [sen-chi], which can also be used in this situation.

짧게 잘라 주세요. [jjal-kke jal-la ju-se-yo.] : Please cut it short.

The word **짧게** means "short" and **잘라 주세요** means "please cut"; therefore, to indicate where you would like it short, you can point to the part you would like short and say **여기** [yeo-gi].

(앞머리) 잘라 주세요. [am-meo-ri jal-la ju-se-yo.] : Please cut my (bangs).

앞머리 can be replaced with several words. See the list of nouns below for different sections of hair in Korean.

Sections of Hair

앞머리 [am-meo-ri]　　　　hair in front; bangs

옆머리 [yeom-meo-ri]　　　the side of the head

옆에 [yeo-pe]　　　　　　the side(s)

뒷머리 [dwin-meo-ri]　　　the back of the head

뒤에 [dwi-e]　　　　　　　the back

위에 [wi-e]　　　　　　　the top

구렛나루 [gu-ren-na-ru]　　sideburns
　　　　　　　　　　　　* This is the colloquial version. The correct term is
　　　　　　　　　　　　구레나룻 [gu-re-na-rut].

자르지 마세요. [ja-reu-ji ma-se-yo.] : Don't cut it, please.

For any phrase that uses "**잘라 주세요** [jal-la ju-se-yo]", you can also use "**자르지 마세요**", meaning "please don't cut", if you want to leave a portion of your hair untouched.

Sample Sentences

앞머리는 **자르지 마세요**. [am-meo-ri-neun ja-reu-ji ma-se-yo.] = Don't cut the bangs/fringe.

옆머리는 **자르지 마세요**. [yeom-meo-ri-neun ja-reu-ji ma-se-yo.] = Don't cut the sides (of the head).

너무 많이 **자르지 마세요**. [neo-mu ma-ni ja-reu-ji ma-se-yo.] = Don't cut too much.

밀어 주세요. [mi-reo ju-se-yo.] : Please shave it.

This phrase means "please shave it", but "it" must be clarified. Add **다** [da] to the front of the phrase to mean "please shave everything" and add **옆머리** [yeom-meo-ri] to the front of the phrase to mean "please shave the sides".

Sample Sentences

옆머리 **밀어 주세요**. [yeom-meo-ri mi-reo ju-se-yo.] = Please shave the sides (of the head).

다 **밀어 주세요**. [da mi-reo ju-se-yo.] = Please shave everything.

(그냥) 다듬어 주세요. [(geu-nyang) da-deu-meo ju-se-yo.] : Just trim it, please.

This is a useful phrase for going to a stylist who knows your specific hair preference. You can also use this phrase with a hairstylist that you've never gone to, but results will vary.

사진 좀 보여 주세요. [sa-jin jom bo-yeo ju-se-yo.] : Please show me some photos (of different hair styles).

If you're unsure of what kind of hairstyle you would like, most hair salons have style books with pictures of trendy hairstyles to choose from.

Hair stylists should ask the following phrases before making any cuts to your bangs or fringe:

앞머리 다듬어 드릴까요? [am-meo-ri da-deu-meo deu-ril-kka-yo?] : Do you want me to trim your bangs/fringe?
앞머리 기르실 건가요? [am-meo-ri gi-reu-sil geon-ga-yo?] : Will you grow your bangs?

You can reply by saying, "네" [ne], which means "yes, I want to grow out my bangs", or "아니요" [a-ni-yo], meaning "no, I don't want to grow out my bangs". To be even clearer, another way to reply is, "잘라 주세요" [jal-la ju-se-yo], which translates to "please cut it", or "자르지 마세요" [ja-reu-ji ma-se-yo], meaning "please don't cut it".

머리 감겨 드릴게요. [meo-ri gam-gyeo deu-ril-kke-yo.] / 샴푸 해 드릴게요. [syam-pu hae deu-ril-kke-yo.] : Let me wash your hair.

The first phrase is the native Korean phrase for washing one's hair. However, the English word "shampoo" is the same in Korean and can be easily understood.

드라이 해 드릴게요. [deu-ra-i hae deu-ril-kke-yo.] : **I'll blow dry your hair.**

The word **드라이**, "dry", is a shortened version of the English phrase "blow dry" and is used to mean the same. This should be announced after hair washing.

머릿결이 많이 상하셨네요. [meo-rit-kkyeo-ri ma-ni sang-ha-syeon-ne-yo.] : **You hair is quite damaged.**

After examining the status of your hair, a stylist may suggest certain treatments to improve the quality of your hair.

Here are more phrases you may hear when your stylist asks you to do certain things, such as checking yourself in the mirror, turning your head, etc.

거울로 한번 봐 보세요. [geo-ul-lo han-beon bwa bo-se-yo.] : **Please look at the mirror and see if you like it.**

이 정도면 됐나요? [i jeong-do-myeon dwaen-na-yo?] : **Is this enough?**

고개 이쪽으로 돌려 주세요. [go-gae i-jjo-geu-ro dol-lyeo ju-se-yo.] : **Please turn your head this way.**

고개 숙여 주세요. [go-gae su-gyeo ju-se-yo.] : **Please look down.**

고개 들어 주세요. [go-gae deu-reo ju-se-yo.] : **Please look up.**

안경 벗어 주세요. [an-gyeong beo-seo ju-se-yo.] : **Please take off your glasses.**

Here are a few words that describe different types of hair:

생머리 [saeng-meo-ri] : straight hair

Although the correct pronunciation of this word is [saeng-meo-ri] (생머리), in reality, people pronounce it as [ssaeng-meo-ri] (쌩머리).

곱슬머리 [gop-sseul-meo-ri] : (naturally) curly hair
반곱슬 [ban-gop-sseul] : wavy

반곱슬 literally means "half curly" and is used to describe wavy hair. The colloquial pronunciation of this word is 반꼽슬 [ban-kkop-seul], which is slightly different than the way it is spelled.

BREAK TIME

Korean Hair vs. Non-Korean Hair

Many Korean stylists do not have any experience with non-Korean (non-Asian) hair, so when encountering different types of hair, sometimes the stylist is unsure of how to handle the situation. Hair types that are not common in Korea include afro-textured hair, fine/thin hair, coily hair, and a few others. To avoid any problems, many non-Asian expats seek out hair stylists that have experience with their hair types. This type of information is commonly shared on the Internet.

Amenities

Many hair salons in Korea offer free drinks when you are waiting for the next available stylist or for when treatments take time to settle. Larger hair salon chains have their own baristas, and some even have an entire cafe area attached to the salon. In addition, there are usually computers that are free to use for any waiting customer. Many hair salons also offer discounts with membership cards and rewards for repeat customers with point cards, such as 10% off every ₩100,000 spent.

TICKETS

티켓 [ti-ket] / 표 [pyo] : ticket

티켓 and 표 are both understood equally. However, most people use the Korean word 표 when being more specific.

영화 [yeong-hwa] : movie

영화표 [yeong-hwa-pyo]: movie ticket

기차 [gi-cha] : train

기차표 [gi-cha-pyo]: train ticket

비행기 [bi-haeng-gi] : airplane

비행기표 [bi-haeng-gi-pyo]: plane ticket

연극 [yeon-geuk] : theatrical performance, play

연극표 [yeon-geuk-pyo]: ticket for play or theater performance

성인 [seong-in] : adult
학생 [hak-ssaeng] : student
어린이 [eo-ri-ni] : child(ren)

Some tickets, such as movie tickets or amusement park tickets, will have different prices for adults, students, and children.

(number) + - 장 주세요. [(number) + - jang ju-se-yo.] : Please give me (number) ticket(s).

This phrase can be used for any number of tickets. Add the word **장** to the number of tickets desired and add **주세요** at the end. Let's take a look at adding on words for specific types of tickets below.

Sample Sentences

한 **장** 주세요. [han jang ju-se-yo.] = Please give me one ticket.

두 **장** 주세요. [du jang ju-se-yo.] = Please give me two tickets.

다섯 **장** 주세요. [da-seot jjang ju-se-yo.] = Please give me five tickets.

AT THE MOVIES

(movie title), (time) + (number) + - 장 주세요. [(title), (time) + (number) + - jang ju-se-yo.] : Please give me (number) ticket(s) for (movie title) at (time).

For movie tickets, add the movie title and time of movie to the front of the phrase.

1시 30분 [han-si-sam-sip-ppun]: 1:30

2시 25분 [du-si-i-si-bo-bun]: 2:25

7시 반 [il-gop-ssi ban]: 7:30

8시 [yeo-deol-ssi]: 8:00

Sample Sentences

겨울왕국 4시 2장 주세요. [gyeo-ul-wang-guk ne-si du-jang ju-se-yo.] = Please give me two tickets for "Frozen" at four o'clock.

변호인 3시 5장 주세요. [byeon-ho-in se-si da-seot-jjang ju-se-yo.] = Please give me five tickets for "The Attorney" at three o'clock.

인셉션 11시 1장 주세요. [in-ssep-ssyeon yeol-han-si han-jang ju-se-yo.] = Please give me one ticket for "Inception" at eleven o'clock.

예매 [ye-mae] : reservation

Movie tickets can be purchased and reserved in advance using smartphone applications or websites. These tickets can be retrieved through the ticketing machines found in every movie theater, many of which have the option for English instructions.

좌석을 선택해 주세요. [jwa-seo-geul seon-tae-kae ju-se-yo.] : Please choose your seat(s).

Korean movie theaters use assigned seating and ask patrons to select their seats before entering the theater. Making reservations has an advantage because you are able to select seats in advance. Movie-goers that buy tickets shortly before a movie are assigned leftover seats which is usually not the best for viewing the movie.

AMUSEMENT PARK

자유 이용권 [ja-yu i-yong-kkwon] : all-access pass

At amusement parks, you typically have two options: pay the minimum entrance fee and pay for each ride you get on, or buy an all-access pass and enjoy an unlimited number of rides and shows. The **자유 이용권** have separate prices for adults and children. Some parks may also have a special discount price for students.

TRAIN

There are several train types (not subways) in Korea, each with differing travel times and pricing. You can make reservations for your train tickets using the official Korail mobile application or online, and once you have been assigned a seat number, you don't have to show your ticket or seat number to anyone the entire duration of the train ride. The staff will regularly check and compare ticket sales records with where passengers are sitting to confirm empty seats.

KTX [ke-i-ti-ek-sseu] : Korean Train eXpress

KTX is the newest and fastest railway in South Korea. It regularly travels above 200 kph (about 124 mph). It is, however, the most expensive of the three main train types. The estimated time from Seoul to Busan on the KTX is 2 hours 45 minutes.

새마을호 [sae-ma-eul-ho] : Saemaeul Train

The Saemaeul Train has more comfortable seating than its older cousin, the Mugunghwa train, and has no room for standing passengers. It is only marginally faster than the Mugunghwa Train for a slightly higher price. The estimated time from Seoul to Busan on the Saemaeul is 5 hours.

무궁화호 [mu-gung-hwa-ho] : Mugunghwa Train

The Mungunghwa Train is the oldest train line and is also the most affordable. The train has both seats and standing room, which is the most affordable option for any railway travel. Many rural stations are serviced exclusively by this train. The estimated travel time from Seoul to Busan on the Mugunghwa is 5 hours, 20 minutes.

The following are more useful vocabulary words related to train rides:

More Words

승차권 [seung-cha-kkwon]	boarding ticket (for train or bus)
왕복 [wang-bok]	round-trip
편도 [pyeon-do]	one-way trip
출발 [chul-bal]	departure
도착 [do-chak]	arrival
발권 [bal-kkwon]	issuing one's ticket

When you buy your train ticket, you may be asked to choose between the following two options:

순방향 [sun-bang-hyang] : forward-facing seating
역방향 [yeok-ppang-hyang] : rear-facing seating

The KTX trains have seats that face both the front and the back of the train. The majority of travelers prefer forward-facing seats which tend to sell out quicker. There is a set of four seats in the middle of each train car, in each row, with two front-facing seats and two rear-facing seats, all of which can be reserved for a cheaper price.

THEATER / CONCERT

(time/date) + 티켓 (number) + - 장 주세요. [(time/date) ti-ket ~jang ju-se-yo.] : Please give me (number) ticket(s) for (time).

For concerts and theatrical performances, add the word 티켓 after the time and date of the desired show. If you are purchasing at the ticket gate, the time and date are usually unnecessary (unless you are reserving in advance) as there is typically only one performance a day.

Sample Sentences

3시 티켓 두 장 주세요. [se-si ti-ket du jang ju-se-yo.] = Please give me two tickets for the play/concert at three o'clock.

8시 티켓 한 장 주세요. [yeo-deol-ssi ti-ket han-jang ju-se-yo.] = Please give me one ticket for the play/concert at eight o'clock.

1월 20일 티켓 두 장 주세요. [i-rwol-i-si-bil ti-ket du jang ju-se-yo.] = Please give me two tickets for the play/concert for January 20.

12월 24일 티켓 두 장 주세요. [si-bi-wol i-sip-ssa-il ti-ket du-jang ju-se-yo.]: Please give me two tickets for the play/concert for December 24.

(name of the seat) + - 석 주세요. [(name of the seat) + - seok ju-se-yo.] : Please give me the (name of the seat) seat.

Seat in Korean is 좌석 [jwa-seok], and when you talk about a specific type of seat, only the second letter (석) is used. For certain events, typically at larger capacity venues, there are different types of seats at different price ranges. These are typically priced from most expensive to least expensive in the following order:

VIP석 [beu-i-a-i-pi-seok] : VIP seat (the best seat)

VIP seats are the best seats in the venue. Sometimes, VVIP tickets are also available. These are the closest to the performance and sometimes include special access areas such as backstage or a lounge area.

R석 [al-seok] : the second best seat

R석, or "R seats", are usually the second closest to the performance. R stands for "royal".

S석 [e-seu-seok] : the third best seat

S석, or "S seats", are the third tier of seating. S stands for "special".

일반석 [il-ban-seok] : regular seat

Some venues also have "regular seats", which are the most inexpensive seats available.

BREAK TIME

How to buy tickets

For movie tickets, some people go to the theater and buy tickets in person or through an automated ticket machine (which has non-Korean menu options). Movies are often sold out and most reservations are done (days) in advance through smartphone applications (which do not have English options). Reserving for theater, concert, or sports tickets is typically done through interpark.com, Korea's top ticket issuing website, which has English in addition to other languages.

KR Pass

KR Pass is a one-price unlimited travel train pass exclusively for foreigners. Passes are available in one, three, five, seven, or ten day options, during which you can use all trains, including KTX. KR Pass can be reserved at korail.com (click the English button on top of the webpage). Follow the links for KR Pass and make a reservation online. This e-ticket must be redeemed at a major train station in Korea, such as Seoul Station.

Unique Movie Experiences

Many theaters in Korea have 4D movies. If you have not experienced 4D before, imagine a 3D movie with the addition of moving seats, water misters, wind, fragrance, and much more! These additions really make you "feel" as if you are part of the scene and provide a truly unique experience.

Korea is home to one of the largest movie screens in the world, CGV Starium, found in the Time Square Mall (**타임스퀘어** [ta-im-seu-kwe-eo]) of Yeongdeungpo (**영등포** [yeong-deung-po]), Seoul. There are also theaters with private dining options, couple seating, high quality headphones, and more.

BANKING

통장 만들고 싶어요. [tong-jang man-deul-go si-peo-yo.] : I would like to open a bank account.

통장 is the word for "bank book", but it also can be used to refer to bank accounts. Although opening a bank account with a passport is possible, you may not have all the options available to you that a legal resident or Korea. As an expat, the most important form of identification that will allow you to open a bank account with full benefits (among other things) is an Alien Registration Card (ARC).

체크 카드 [che-keu ka-deu] : debit card

Check cards, also known as debit cards, are cards that withdraw funds directly from connected bank accounts. They can be used to retrieve cash from an ATM machine, at stores that accept credit cards, and on the Internet. Some check cards, depending on the type of card, cannot be used online or abroad. Don't be afraid to ask the bank about card usability before you decide which card to get.

직불 카드 [jik-ppul ka-deu] : cash card

These cards are more limited than check cards and only allow cash to be withdrawn from ATMs.

신용 카드 [si-nyong ka-deu] : credit card

Credit cards are often difficult for foreigners to obtain because many do not plan for long term residency. There are credit cards available for foreigners, but with many requirements. If the requirements are not met, cards are also available with a deposit, known as 보증금 [bo-jeung-geum]. With a deposit, the card cannot be used as a true credit card. You will still be allowed to make purchases on the Internet and take advantage of the automated and planned payments that check cards usually do not allow.

비밀번호 [bi-mil-beon-ho] : password

비밀 번호 literally means "secret number", and banks will often have customers create passwords for bank accounts. In addition to ATMs and Internet banking, this password is often required for in-person banking activities.

교통 카드 기능 넣어 드릴까요? [gyo-tong ka-deu gi-neung neo-eo deu-ril-kka-yo?] : Shall I add the transportation card function?
교통 카드 기능 넣어 주세요. [gyo-tong ka-deu gi-neung neo-eo ju-se-yo] : Please add the transportation card function.

교통 카드 is a transportation card that you can use for public transportation. Check cards and credit cards can also be used as transportation cards. This should be explicitly stated when creating your card. Instead of pre-paying for transportation, these cards will often charge or deduct the month's transportation fare at the end of the month.
Some banks, such as 신한은행 [sin-ha-neun-haeng] (Shinhan Bank), do not extend this service to foreign customers.

송금 [song-geum] : wire transfer
돈 보내고 싶어요. [don bo-nae-go si-peo-yo.] : I'd like to send money.

송금 is the noun for "wire transfer" or "remittance". Domestic wire transfers, 국내 송금 [gung-nae song-geum], are mostly free of charge and are instantaneous (see tip below). Transfers can be done on smartphones quite easily. For international wire transfers, 국제 송금 [guk-jje song-geum], however, there are numerous fees.

돈 찾고 싶어요. [don chat-kko si-peo-yo.] : I want to withdraw some money.

This phrase literally means "I want to find money", but is often used to tell bank tellers or employees that you would like to withdraw money from your account. If you go to a bank and someone (usually the security guard) asks you what you want to do, use this phrase to tell him/her that you need some cash and you will be pointed in the appropriate direction.

환전 [hwan-jeon] : **currency exchange**

환율 [hwan-nyul] : **exchange rate**

환전해 주세요. [hwan-jeo-nae ju-se-yo.] / 돈 바꿔 주세요. [don ba-kkwo ju-se-yo.] : **Please exchange my currency./Please change my money.**

This phrase can be used at banks as well as currency exchange shops.

To be more specific, use the following:

(currency) + -(으)로 바꿔 주세요. [(currency) eu-ro ba-kkwo ju-se-yo.] : Please change to...

미국 달러로 바꿔 주세요. [mi-guk ttal-leo-ro ba-kkwo ju-se-yo.] : Please change to American dollars.

원으로 바꿔 주세요. [wo-neu-ro ba-kkwo ju-se-yo.] : Please change to (Korean) won.

Other currencies:

원 [won]	Won
미국 달러 [mi-guk ttal-leo]	American Dollar
홍콩 달러 [hong-kong dal-leo]	Hong Kong Dollar
싱가포르 달러 [sing-ga-po-reu dal-leo]	Singaporean Dollar
캐나다 달러 [kae-na-da dal-leo]	Canadian Dollar
파운드 [pa-un-deu]	Pound
유로 [yu-ro]	Euro
엔 [en]	Yen
페소 [pe-so]	Peso
중국 위안 [jung-guk wi-an]	Yuan

뭐 하러 오셨어요? [mwo ha-reo o-syeoss-eo-yo?] : What are you here for?

번호표 뽑고 기다려 주세요. [beo-no-pyo ppop-kko gi-da-ryeo ju-se-yo.] : Please take a number and wait.

These two phrases are most likely to be heard upon entering a bank. A bank employee, usually the security guard, will guide you to a ticket dispenser, some of which have touch screens so you can pick choose the reason you are there and get a ticket. If the machine is not touch screen, the security guard may ask why you are at the bank. Upon answering, the guard will guide you to take a number from the correct machine so you don't end up at the wrong counter (different services are served at different desks in Korean banks). Most banks ask this question because some people might be there for services that are provided in a separate section of the bank, such as getting a loan.

Sample Dialogue

Bank Staff: 뭐 하러 오셨어요? [mwo ha-reo o-syeo-ss-eo-yo?] = What are you here for?

Customer: 통장 만들고 싶어요. [tong-jang man-deul-go si-peo-yo.] = I want to open an account.

Bank Staff: 번호표 뽑고 기다려 주세요. [beo-no-pyo ppop-kko gi-da-ryeo ju-se-yo] = Please take a number and wait.

싸인해 주세요. [ssa-in-hae ju-se-yo.] : **Please sign.**

In addition to signatures, many people have their own personalized stamps, or **도장** [do-jang]. These are legally recognized as signatures and are used for various types of official documents.

여기 ATM 있어요? [yeo-gi e-i-ti-e mi-sseo-yo?] : **Is there an ATM here?**
현금 인출기 어디에 있어요? [hyeon-geum in-chul-gi eo-di-e i-sseo-yo?] : **Where is the ATM?**

ATM is the term for an Automated Teller Machines; however, the older and native Korean term **현금 인출기** is sometimes used instead.

주소 [ju-so] : address

Addresses in Korea are written from general to specific, starting from the city or the province.

Example:
서울시 마포구 서교동 456-78 행복 빌라 901호 [Seo-ul-si ma-po-gu seo-gyo-dong sa-o-yuk-da-si-chil-pal haeng-bok- bil-la gu-bae-gil-ho] = Seoul, Mapo-gu, Seogyeo-dong 456-78 Haengbok Villa #901
경상남도 진주시 상대동 대한 아파트 103동 201호 [gyeong-sang-nam-do jin-ju-si sang-dae-dong dae-han a-pae-teu baek-sam-dong i-bae-gil-ho] = Gyeongsangnam-do, Jinji-si, Sangdae-dong, Daehan Apartments, Building #103, Apartment #201

전화번호 [jeo-nwa-beo-no] : phone number
핸드폰 번호 [haen-deu-pon beo-no] : mobile phone number

Most mobile phone numbers in Korea start with 010. 전화번호 can mean both home phone and mobile phone number. Normally, you provide your mobile phone number for paperwork in banks since, often times, you will receive text messages for any alerts related to your account.
핸드폰 is a Konglish word that derived from a combination of the English words "hand" and "phone". It now means "mobile phone" in Korean.

Sample Sentences

여기에 주소 써 주세요. [yeo-gi-e ju-so sseo-ju-se-yo.] = Please write down your address here.
여기에 전화번호 써 주세요. [yeo-gi-e jeo-nwa-beo-no sseo ju-se-yo.] = Please write down your phone number here.
여기에 핸드폰 번호 써 주세요. [yeo-gi-e haen-deu-pon beo-no sseo ju-se-yo.] = Please write down your mobile number here.

BREAK TIME

Exchanging Currency

Banks will offer currency exchange at standard rates. However, more favorable exchange rates are often found outside of the banks. These can be found at currency exchange booths in popular tourist areas such as Myeongdong, Itaewon, or near military bases. The best rates, however, are offered inside shoe repair stands (in Myeongdong and Itaewon). Also, Namdaemun Market has a group of elderly ladies (near the tourism help booth in the center of the market) that are rumored to have the best rates in Seoul!

Money Transfers

Sending wire transfers among friends and business associates is a common practice since the process is instantaneous and usually free of any fees regardless of which banks are involved. Friends will often agree to pay each other back using wire transfers, and work related payments are also done in this matter as well.

Internet Banking

Utilizing Internet banking requires several security measures. One of the most common forms of security is the use of security keys that are often stored on home computers or portable USB drives that can be used on other computers. These security measures require Microsoft operating systems (OSX and Linux are incompatible for Internet banking). Fortunately, Internet banking is also available on smartphones, which are easier to use than on computers and are more foreigner friendly. Banks have varying policies regarding mobile or Internet banking, so be sure to ask when you can start using these services!

MOBILE PHONE

BUYING A PHONE

스마트폰 보여 주세요. [seu-ma-teu-pon bo-yeo ju-se-yo.] : **Please show me the smartphones (you have).**

By replacing 스마트폰, "smartphone", with the item you are looking for, this phrase can be used in any shopping situation.

(name of the phone) + - 있어요? [(name of the phone) + i-sseo-yo?] : Do you have (name of the phone)?

If you have a specific phone that you are looking for, you may use this phrase to be more specific. It can also be used in other general shopping situations when looking for a specific item.

Sample Sentences

아이폰 7 있어요? [a-i-pon sse-beun i-sseo-yo?] = Do you have the iPhone 7?

갤럭시 노트 6 있어요? [gael-leok-ssi no-teu ssik-sseu i-sseo-yo?] = Do you have the Galaxy Note 6?

외국인 등록증 갖고 계세요? [oe-gu-gin deung-nok-jjeung gat-kko gye-se-yo?] : **Do you have your foreigner registration card?**

외국인 등록증 보여 주세요. [oe-gu-gin deung-nok-jjeung bo-yeo ju-se-yo.] : **Please show me your foreigner registration card.**

In order to sign up for a phone in Korea, you will need an Alien Registration Card (ARC). This card is an ID card given to foreign residents of Korea with a unique ID number. Without this card, it is very difficult to get a phone with a plan or a bank account.

어떤 요금제 쓰실 거예요? [eo-tteon yo-geum-je sseu-sil kkeo-ye-yo?] : Which plan would you like to use?

Korean telecommunications companies have several different plans for call times, data, and text messaging. Many of these plans are two year contracts which include the price of the phone.

개통은 한 시간 정도 후에 될 거예요. [gae-tong-eun han si-gan jeong-do hu-e doel kkeo-ye-yo.] : Your phone should be ready to use after an hour.

The word 개통 refers to the activation of the service or network and is almost exclusively used in this context (buying a cellphone and having it connected to the network system) or in regards to cable Internet service.

첫 세 달만 이 요금제 쓰시고 그 다음부터는 원하시는 요금제로 바꾸시면 돼요. [cheot se dal-man i yo-geum-je sseu-si-go geu da-eum-bu-teo-neun won-ha-si-neun yo-geum-je-ro ba-kku-si-myeon dwae-yo.] : Use this plan for the first three months, and after that, you can switch to the plan you would like.

This is common when buying a phone during a special promotional deal. The typical deal requires you to sign up for a certain plan (usually more expensive than one you actually need) for the first three months. After the initial three months, you are allowed to switch plans.

More Words

데이터 [de-i-teo]	data
통신사 [tong-sin-sa]	carrier

심카드 [sim-ka-deu]	sim card
3G [sseu-ri-ji]	3G
4G [po-ji] / **LTE** [el-ti-i]	4G
약정 [yak-jjeong]	contract
기계값 [gi-gye-kkap]	the price of the device
에그 [e-geu]	"egg", a portable WiFi device
렌탈폰 [ren-tal-pon]	rental phone

ON THE PHONE

여보세요. [yeo-bo-se-yo.] : **(on the phone) Hello.**

"Hello" in Korean is **안녕하세요** [an-nyeong-ha-se-yo], but when answering the phone, the phrase used is "**여보세요?**", not **안녕하세요**.

저 (name) + -이에요/예요. [jeo (name) + -i-e-yo/ye-yo.] : **This is (name).**

잘 안 들려요. [jal an deul-lyeo-yo.] : **I can't hear you clearly.**

잘 들리세요? [jal deul-li-se-yo?] : **Can you hear me clearly?**

제가 지금 바빠서 조금 이따 전화 드릴게요. [je-ga ji-geum ba-ppa-seo jo-geum i-tta jeo-nwa deu-ril-kke-yo.] : **I'm busy right now, so I will call you back later.**

잘못 거신 거 같아요. [jal-mot geo-sin geo ga-ta-yo.] : **I think you have the wrong number.**

BREAK TIME

Texting Applications

Texting in Korea is dominated by KakaoTalk, a chatting application for smartphones that gives users the ability to text message each other for free (by using data). Users can enter group chat windows and check whether or not text messages have been read. There is also a free call function that allows users to make free calls using data. Since this application relies on data, KakaoTalk can also be used if WiFi is available, even if the phone in use is not connected to data service. Friends of friends are suggested as possible contacts to add, and users can also search people by KakaoTalk ID.

Hanging Up

Many phone conversations in Korean are ended without saying "goodbye". Instead, when a conversation is nearing its end, both parties will often exchange "OK" or "yes" a few times before it is clear that both parties will hang up. In Korean, the words used are 네 [ne], the formal way of saying "yes", or 응 [eung], the informal way of saying "yes". Other conversations end by saying "I'm hanging up" (끊을게 [kkeu-neul-kke]), which is used more for intimate relationships.

Spam

Spam is a problem for many mobile phone users in Korea. Some people receive several messages a day asking if they are interested in services. Many times the spam messages and phone calls are related to loans (대출 [dae-chul]) or gambling (도박 [do-bak]). While there are several options for blocking numbers, many times these measures cannot battle all the spam that is sent. Sometimes this is caused by the phone number's previous owner who had presumably requested such information.

PACKAGE DELIVERY

RECEIVING A PACKAGE

택배 [taek-ppae] : delivery / package

택배 아저씨 [taek-ppae-a-jeo-ssi] : delivery man

Since most package deliverers are men, the general term to address an older male, 아저씨, is used.

Sample Sentences

택배 아저씨 왔어요? [taek-ppae a-jeo-ssi wa-sseo-yo?] = Did the delivery man come?

택배 왔어요? [taek-ppae wa-sseo-yo?] = Did I receive a package?

(time) + -전에/이후에 와 주실 수 있어요? [(time) + -jeo-ne/i-hu-e wa ju-sil ssu i-sseo-yo?] : Can you come before/after (time)?

Deliveries in Korea cannot be requested to arrive at specific times, but the delivery men are often asked to come before/after a certain hour. When placing an order, it is best to write this phrase in the space for special instructions. If you forget to include this and your package comes when you're not home, the delivery man will call the phone number you provided, and you can then use this phrase. Depending on the delivery service company or the delivery person's schedule, the deliverer might not be able to come back to the neighborhood again just for you alone, so it is best to let them know beforehand.

Sample Sentences

세 시 이후에 와 주실 수 있어요? [se si i-hu-e wa ju-sil ssu i-sseo-yo?] = Can you come after 3:00?

저녁 일곱 시 이후에 와 주실 수 있어요? [jeo-nyeok il-gop si i-hu-e wa ju-sil ssu i-sseo-yo?] = Can you come after seven in the evening?

열두 시 반 전에 와 주실 수 있어요? [yeol-du si ban jeo-ne wa ju-sil ssu i-sseo-yo?] = Can you come before 12:30?

경비실에 맡겨 주세요. [gyeong-bi-si-re mat-kkyeo ju-se-yo.] : Please leave it at the security desk.

Most homes in big cities in Korea are apartments rather than stand-alone homes. Many apartment buildings/complexes have a security desk and security guards, which makes this phrase the most common instruction for deliveries. Use this phrase when a delivery man calls to deliver your package and you are not at home to receive it.

문 앞에 놔 주세요. [mun a-pe nwa ju-se-yo.] : Please leave it in front of the door.

If you live in a building that has a separate entrance door to the building that only residents can open, you can safely tell the delivery person to leave the package in front of your building entrance.

택배입니다. [taek-ppae-im-ni-da.] / 택배인데요. [taek-ppae-in-de-yo.] : (this is a) delivery/package

When delivering a package, delivery men will say either of these two phrases through the door or phone.

지금 집에 안 계셔서 전화드렸어요. [ji-geum ji-be an gye-syeo-seo jeon-nwa-deu-ryeo-sseo-yo.] : I'm calling you because you are not at home now.

This phrase is often the first phrase the delivery man says when calling you.

집에 계세요? [ji-be gye-se-yo?] : Are you at home (now)?
집에 언제 계세요? [ji-be eon-je gye-se-yo?] : When are you home?

You'll hear this phrase when a delivery man is calling before arriving at your home.

(time) + 이따 후에 갈게요. [(time) + i-tta/hu-e gal-kke-yo.] : I will be there in (time).

This phrase is said after you confirm that you are home and the delivery is on its way.

Sample Sentences

10분 후에 갈게요. [sip-ppun hu-e- gal-kke-yo.] = I'll be there in 10 minutes.

30분 이따 갈게요. [sam-sip-ppun i -tta gal-kke-yo.] = I'll be there in 30 minutes.

1시간 후에 갈게요. [han-si-gan hu-e gal-kke-yo.] = I'll be there in one hour.

Sample Dialogue

(On the phone)

Delivery: **택배인데요.** [taek-ppae-in-de-yo.] **집에 계세요?** [ji-be gye-se-yo?] = Delivery. Are you at home?

You: **아니요.** [a-ni-yo.] **지금 집 아닌데요.** [ji-geum jip a-nin-de-yo.] = I'm not at home now.

Delivery: **집에 언제 계세요?** [ji-be eon-je gye-se-yo?] = When are you at home?

You: **7시 이후에 와 주실 수 있어요?** [il-gop-ssi i-hu-e wa ju-sil ssu i-sseo-yo?] = Can you come after seven?

(On the phone)

Delivery: **택배인데요.** [taek-ppae-in-de-yo.] **지금 집에 안 계셔서 전화드렸어요.** [ji-geum ji-be an gye-syeo-seo jeo-nwa deu-ryeo-sseo-yo.] = Delivery. I'm calling you because you are not at home.

You: **집 앞 편의점에 맡겨 주세요.** [jip ap pyeo-nui-jeo-me mat-kkyeo ju-se-yo.] = Please leave it at the convenience store in front of the house

SENDING A PACKAGE (AT THE POST OFFICE)

어디 보내시는 거예요? [eo-di bo-nae-si-neun geo-ye-yo?] : Where are you sending it to?

The post office employee may ask you this question after you have filled out the appropriate forms and present him/her with your package.

(country)(city in Korea) + -에 보내는 거예요. [(country)(city in Korea) + -e bo-nae-neun geo-ye-yo.] : I'm sending it to (country)(city in Korea).

When replying, you can simply state the country or city in Korea that you are sending it to, but using this entire phrase will make it complete and more polite.

Sample Sentences

미국에 보내는 거예요. [mi-gu-ge bo-nae-neun geo-ye-yo.] = I'm sending it to the U.S.

싱가포르에 보내는 거예요. [sing-ga-po-reu-e bo-nae-neun geo-ye-yo.] = I'm sending it to Singapore.

캐나다에 보내는 거예요. [kae-na-da-e bo-nae-neun geo-ye-yo.] = I'm sending it to Canada.

부산에 보내는 거예요. [bu-sa-ne bo-nae-neun geo-ye-yo.] = I'm sending it to Busan.

뭐 들었어요? [mwo deu-reo-sseo-yo?] : What's in it?

List the package contents on the form provided. This can be done in English.

박스 하나 주세요. [bak-sseu ha-na ju-se-yo] : Please give me one box.

Post offices sell boxes of different sizes at inexpensive prices. If you don't have a box for your package, you can buy one and pack it at the post office.

깨지기 쉬운 물건이에요. [kkae-ji-gi swi-un mul-geo-ni-e-yo.] : It's a fragile package.

If your package is fragile, inform the worker at the post office so that your package is labeled and handled appropriately.

얼마나 걸려요? [eol-ma-na geol-lyeo-yo?] : How long will it take?

Post office employees can provide estimates of how long it will take to reach the final destination after calculating the weight and delivery method. The EMS (express) service provides text message alerts to inform customers where the packages are, when it is expected to be delivered, and whether or not it has been successfully delivered.

3일 [sa-mil]: 3 days

1주(일) [il-ju(-il)]: 1 week

2주(일) [i-ju(-il)]: 2 weeks

2달 [du-dal]: 2 months

일반 [il-ban] : regular
EMS [i-e-me-sseu] : express

These are the two basic delivery services. The time and price difference can be substantial, so if price is an issue, be sure to ask before filling out the forms.

제일 빠른 걸로 보내 주세요. [je-il ppa-reun geol-lo bo-nae ju-se-yo.] : Please send it the quickest way possible.

Obviously this will be a more expensive delivery method. It can be months faster than the slowest/cheapest option.

제일 싼 걸로 보내 주세요. [je-il ssan geol-lo bo-nae ju-se-yo.] : Please send it the cheapest way possible.

For larger and heavier packages, the price difference between express and regular deliveries can be quite big.

우표 [u-pyo] : **stamp**

Stamps are used mostly for domestic mail and can be purchased at post offices.

175

서류 봉투 [seo-ryu bong-tu] : **document envelope**

If you are sending a document, this is the type of envelope that is most commonly used.

송장 번호 [song-jang beo-no] : **tracking number**

Depending on the type of package, the destination, as well service used, the post office can provide tracking numbers on receipts. The Korea Post website is in English, and tracking numbers can be entered there. (Korea Post English website - http://www.koreapost.go.kr/eng/). Smaller packages and documents are usually untrackable unless sent with express service (EMS).

BREAK TIME

Online Shopping

When ordering items from the Internet, the checkout page usually has an entry field for delivery instructions. For most residents with a security guard at their apartment building, the message is most often 경비실에 맡겨 주세요 [gyeong-bi-si-re mat-kkyeo ju-se-yo], "please leave it at the security desk". Specific delivery times (e.g. before/after 2:00) can also be requested, but they cannot always be fulfilled.

Easy Packing

When sending a package, you can simply go to the post office with the items you would like to send along with the address. Everything else is provided at the post office. Boxes of various sizes are sold at the counters for inexpensive prices. The post office will also have tape, scissors, box cutters, and markers so that you and other customers can prepare packages inside the post office.

DATING & MARRIAGE

SETTING UP DATES

밥 먹었어요? [bap meo-geo-sseo-yo?] : Did you eat breakfast/lunch/dinner?

This is a common phrase not just for dating situations, but also day-to-day colloquial Korean. It's akin to the English phrase "how are you?" and, similarly, is used as a greeting. In the past, eating three meals a day was not always guaranteed in Korea, and asking if one has eaten shows care and concern for people's health and well-being.

The following are more phrases you might want to know when it comes to asking someone out on a date or when you are discussing what you want to do together:

먹고 싶은 거 있어요? [meok-kko si-peun geo i-sseo-yo?] : Is there anything you want to eat?

In major cities in Seoul, which is where the majority of both local Korean and expat population live, dates often take place indoors since there are not many public places out in the open that people can go to very easily. Most dates will start by having a meal together, followed by some coffee or tea, then a visit to a shopping or entertainment center, such as a mall or movie theater.

영화 볼래요? [yeong-hwa bol-lae-yo?] : Do you want to go see a movie?

Movies may be the most popular date choice for couples and dates in Korea. Go to any theater on the weekend and there will be couples everywhere. Try to reserve in advance (especially for weekend showings) as movies often are sold out or only seats all the way in the front or to the sides are available without reservations.

무슨 영화 볼래요? [mu-seun yeong-hwa bol-lae-yo?] : **Which movie do you want to see?**

Use the following phrases for making plans and setting up dates in advance:

이번 주말에 시간 있어요? [i-beon ju-ma-re si-gan i-sseo-yo?] : **Do you have time this weekend?**

이번 주말에 뭐 해요? [i-beon ju-ma-re mwo hae-yo?] : **What are you doing this weekend?**

Instead of using **이번 주말**, meaning "this weekend", you can ask what someone is doing next weekend by replacing **이번 주말** with **다음 주말** [da-eum ju-mal] (next weekend).

The following phrases are quite common when you have just met someone. It's a casual phrase that doesn't directly ask someone out on a date, but leaves open the possibility for one. These phrases don't necessarily indicate romantic interest, however, and are just as frequently used when making new friends.

언제 밥 한번 같이 먹어요. [eon-je bap han-beon ga-chi meo-geo-yo.] : **Let's grab a bite together some time.**

언제 커피 한 잔 해요. [eon-je keo-pi han jan hae-yo.] : **Let's have a cup of coffee some time.**

소개팅 할래요? [so-gae-ting hal-lae-yo?] : **Would you like to go on a blind date?**
소개팅 시켜 주세요. [so-gae-ting si-kyeo ju-se-yo.] : **Please set me up with someone.**

Blind dates are very common in Korea and are a big part of the dating culture. As blind dates involve a 3rd party that both parties know, there is a certain level of safety and trust in every blind date, which is part of the reason why blind dates are so popular in Korea. When a blind date is strictly based on the assumption that both participants are looking for someone to marry, it is then called **선** [seon] instead of **소개팅**. **선** is typically set up by the parents or friends of the parents.

WHEN DATING

사랑해요. [sa-rang-hae-yo.] : I love you.

사랑해요 is the respectful way to say "I love you". As many couples are comfortable with each other and don't have many formalities, this type of language may be too formal for some relationships. For a more intimate and non-formal way to say "I love you", drop the last syllable and just say "**사랑해**" [sa-rang-hae].

좋아해요. [jo-a-hae-yo.] : I like you.

This phrase is translated literally as "I like" and can be used to express admiration for many things (foods, colors, songs, etc.) Most times, however, exactly what the speaker is referring to should be clear from the context. To be more specific, you can add the person's name in front, for example, **유빈 씨 좋아해요** [yu-bin ssi jo-a-hae-yo]. Also, as with most phrases in Korean, dropping **요** [yo] from the end of the phrase makes it less formal.

보고 싶어요. [bo-go-si-peo-yo.] : I miss you.

This phrase will most likely be used in text messages, letters, emails, and over the phone. Just as with previous phrases, dropping **요** [yo] from the end of the phrase makes it less formal.

커플링 [keo-peul-ling] : couple rings

Many couples in Korea get matching rings, sometimes with engravings, to show that they are a couple. In addition, many couples also wear matching t-shirts, jackets, shoes, backpacks, etc.

데이트 코스 [de-i-teu ko-sseu] : "date course"

This Konglish phrase refers to a date with several stops. This can include going to a dinner, movie, coffee shop, bar, and more. This phrase is commonly found on the Internet with blogs that suggest certain "date courses".

MARRIAGE

결혼해 줄래? [gyeol-hon-hae jul-lae?] : Will you marry me?
결혼해 줘. [gyeol-hon-hae jwo.] : Marry me.
결혼하자. [gyeol-hon-ha-ja.] : Let's get married.

The first phrase, "**결혼해 줄래?**", asks the person to "marry me" and is the phrase used in most proposals. The second phrase isn't a direct request, but rather more of a suggestion to get married.

상견례 [sang-gyeon-nye] : family meeting

상견례 is the meeting of both the bride's and the groom's family. Once a couple has decided to get married, a **상견례** will be set up for the families to meet each other, usually at a formal dinner. Once the families have met and approved of each other, the wedding will be official and wedding preparations will begin. The date of the wedding will also be discussed or start being discussed on this day.

결혼식 [gyeol-hon-sik] : wedding
청첩장 [cheong-cheop-jjang] : wedding invitation

결혼식장 [gyeol-hon-sik-jjang] / 식장 [sik-jjang] : wedding venue

Wedding ceremonies often take place in hotels, churches, or "wedding halls", which are venues designed specifically for weddings. Many wedding halls are large enough to host several weddings on the same day. Wedding hall staff guide the wedding participants step-by-step, ushering from one room to another and providing exact directions for where to stand and what to do next.

축의금 [chu-gui-geum] : money gift for happy occasions (especially weddings)

The most typical Korean wedding gift is cash. Money is usually prepared in envelopes with the giver's name written on the outside. Most weddings will distribute wedding meal coupons upon receiving these envelopes.

신혼여행 [sin-hon-nyeo-haeng] : honeymoon

For newly married couples that don't want to go too far away for their honeymoon, Jeju Island is the most popular honeymoon destination in Korea. For those traveling outside of Korea, some popular honeymoon destinations for Korean people include Hawaii, Guam, Cebu, Bali, Phuket, Boracay, the Maldives, France, Greece, and Spain.

시어머니 [si-eo-meo-ni] : woman's mother in law
시아버지 [si-a-beo-ji] : woman's father in law
장모님 [jang-mo-nim] : man's mother in law
장인어른 [jang-in-eo-reun] : man's father in law

The terms used for mother-in-law and father-in-law differ according to the speaker's sex. These terms, however, are for referring to a parent-in-law in the third person. When someone is talking directly to a parent-in-law, the honorific form of the words "mother", **어머님** [eo-meo-nim], and "father", **아버님** [a-beo-nim], are used.

BREAK TIME

How Much to Give at Weddings

The typical wedding gift in Korea is cash. Most people give the same amount of money which was received on their own wedding day. For friends and family who have not yet received money from the bride/groom, the amount of money to give is determined by a number of factors, including closeness and type of relationship (family, co-worker/boss, friend, etc.) As odd numbers represent good luck, the amount given should always be in odd numbers with ₩30,000 being the minimum (₩30,000, ₩50,000, ₩70,000, etc.) ₩30,000 is considered the minimum because the average cost for a meal at wedding halls is around ₩30,000. At ₩100,000 and beyond, the odd number rule no longer applies.

Blind Dates in Korea

Although random encounters (at restaurants, bars, etc.) with strangers do happen, some people are leery of this type of meeting because it is sometimes viewed as a casual, non-serious relationship. On the other hand, meeting someone through a blind date, **소개팅** [so-gae-ting], can be more comfortable for some as both parties know a mutual person, and thus, a certain level of trust and safety is implied. Also, most of the time it's assumed that both people on the blind date are looking for something more serious.

A more serious type of blind date is called **선** [seon], which is arranged by parents. Usually the parents know each other and are arranging for their children to meet. These have heavy marriage implications as the families of both parties have already approved of each other. Often, **선** [seon] have very short dating periods since marriage is the main purpose of the blind date.

Korean Couple Culture

Many younger couples in Korea like to wear matching clothes, t-shirts, pants, shoes, backpacks, and even keychains. It is a way for many couples to express their love and dedication to each other as well as to the general public. In addition to yearly anniversaries, some couples celebrate their 100th, 200th, 300th, etc. day anniversary. This, too, is practiced more by younger couples. It is not very common for couples to pay for dates together, it is however more common for one person to take care of the first bill (movie or dinner), and the other person to take care of the second bill (coffee or dessert cafe).

HEALTH

HOSPITAL & PHARMACY

COMMON PHRASES

(body part) + -이/가 아파요. [(body part) + -i/ga a-pa-yo.] : My (body part) hurts.
(body part) + -을/를 다쳤어요. [(body part) + -eul/reul da-cheo-sseo-yo.] : My (body part) hurts.

In Korea, instead of walking through the aisles of a pharmacy to pick up over-the-counter medicine, many people consult with the pharmacists to get medicine. Simply tell the pharmacist your symptoms using one of both of these two phrases, and the pharmacist will go behind the counter and get some medication for you.

These phrases can be also useful in the hospital when speaking to administrative staff or nurses who are less fluent in English and are assessing you before the doctor. Although most doctors in Korea can understand and communicate in English fairly well, the rest of the hospital staff may not.

Sample Sentences

머리가 아파요. [meo-ri-ga a-pa-yo.] = I have a headache.
배가 아파요. [bae-ga a-pa-yo.] = I have a stomachache.
눈이 아파요. [nu-ni a-pa-yo.] = My eyes hurt.

눈을 다쳤어요. [nu-neul da-cheo-sseo-yo.] = I hurt my eye.
다리를 다쳤어요. [da-ri-reul da-cheo-sseo-yo.] = I hurt my leg.
팔을 다쳤어요. [pa-reul da-cheo-sseo-yo.] = I hurt my arm.

Body Parts

배 [bae]   stomach

머리 [meo-ri]   head

눈 [nun]   eye

코 [ko]   nose

입 [ip]   mouth

귀 [gwi]   ear

발 [bal]   foot

손 [son]   hand

The following are phrases for other common symptoms you may need to describe in Korean:

속이 안 좋아요. [so-gi an jo-a-yo.] : I feel nauseous.; I feel bloated. (refers to general discomfort)

열이 나요. [yeo-ri na-yo.] : **I have a fever.**

기침이 나요. [gi-chi-mi na-yo.] : **I have a cough.**

감기에 걸린 것 같아요. [gam-gi-e geol-lin geot ga-ta-yo.] : **I think I've caught a cold.**

토했어요. [to-hae-sseo-yo.] : **I threw up.**

(body part)에서 피가 나요. [pi-ga na-yo.] : **(body part) is bleeding.**

약 [yak] : **medicine**

Common Phrases

The Korean government restricts the distribution of prescription medication strictly to pharmacies. While non-prescription medicine is available at convenience stores or supermarkets, selection and supply are very limited.

처방전 [cheo-bang-jeon] : prescription

Doctors typically prescribe medicine in sufficient amounts for short-term ailments, usually either three days' or a week's worth. In terms of chronic health problems which require regular visits, such as diabetes, as much as one month's worth of medicine can be prescribed. If you believe you need a refill for a prescription, you will have to visit the doctor again for another consultation in order to receive another prescription.

보험 [bo-heom] : insurance

The Korean government requires that all citizens as and foreigner residents be insured, usually through the National Health Insurance, which is typically provided by employers when you put in a percentage of your salary (pre-tax) into the system so you can receive services. In addition to NHI, many people sign up for private-sector insurance services to supplement the social insurance system.

Sample Sentences

보험이 없어요 [bo-heo-mi eop-sseo-yo] = I don't have insurance.

보험 있어요 [bo-heom i-sseo-yo] = I have insurance.

BREAK TIME

한의학 [ha-nui-hak], 한의사 [ha-nui-sa] and 한의원 [ha-nui-won]

Traditional Korean medicine (한의학) is one alternative to consider. Most modern medicine is focused on curing illnesses and diseases, whereas traditional Korean medicine is focused on preventing illnesses and diseases. Traditional Korean medicine utilizes medicinal herbs and roots as well as acupuncture and aromatherapy, among other things.

HOSPITAL

의사 선생님 [ui-sa seon-saeng-nim] : doctor

의사 means "doctor" and 선생님 means " teacher". When you put these two words together, this is one way to address a doctor, but most of the time it is shortened to 선생님.

접수 [jeop-ssu] : reception

Typically at larger hospitals, someone at the front desk will ask you what the problem is and direct you to a specific section of the hospital to receive the proper care.

주사 [ju-sa] : injection, shot
주사실 [ju-sa-sil] : injection room

In Korea, injections in the buttocks are common, even for non–buttock related illnesses such as the flu.

진료 [jil-lyo] : examination

This word refers to when the doctor examines a patient to find the problem.

진료비 [jil-lyo-bi] : hospital bill, medical expense

응급실 [eung-geup-ssil] : emergency room

Emergency rooms in Korea are not private rooms. Instead of walls, there are curtains between beds to offer a bit of privacy. Medical consultation with the doctors often take place with the curtains drawn.

As every resident in Korea is required to be enrolled for the National Health Insurance, health care is relatively affordable for most people, even in emergency rooms. For those uninsured, however, emergency room visits can be as high as ₩200,000 or even higher, depending on the nature of the visit.

증상 [jeung-sang] : symptom

The following are department names in Korea. While large hospitals may have several of these departments in one building, local hospitals may only specialize in one.

Department Names

내과 [nae-kkwa]	internal medicine—akin to general practice
안과 [an-kkwa]	ophthalmology (eyes)
치과 [chi-kkwa]	dental
이비인후과 [i-bi-in-hu-kkwa]	ear, nose, throat
정형외과 [jeong-hyeong-oe-kkwa]	orthopedics
성형외과 [seong-hyeong-oe-kkwa]	plastic surgery
소아과 [so-a-kkwa]	pediatrics

진단서 [jin-dan-seo] : medical certificate, (written) diagnosis; doctor's note

Sometimes, a medical certificate that proves you were in the hospital is necessary for school, work, or insurance. The cost for issuing this document can vary depending on the hospital and can be requested at the reception desk of the hospital.

입원 [i-bwon] : hospitalization

입원하다 [i-bwon-ha-da] is the verb for "to be hospitalized".

퇴원 [toe-won] : discharge (after being hospitalized)

퇴원하다 [toe-won-ha-da] is the verb for "to be discharged (from a hospital)".

입원 치료 [i-bwon chi-ryo] : inpatient treatment

This term refers to getting medical treatment while staying at a hospital. Hospitals have signs that read **입원 치료**, which you can follow and be lead to the rooms where the patients stay.

통원 치료 [tong-won chi-ryo] : outpatient treatment

This term refers to medical care that does not require overnight hospitalization, such as ultrasounds, standard check-ups, lab tests, etc.

수술 [su-sul] : surgery
시술 [si-sul] : medical procedure

수술 normally involves cutting open a certain body part, whereas **시술** usually refers to any treatment that only involve injections or very small cuts.

링거 [ling-geo] : IV (intravenous line)

Administering a saline IV is common practice in Korea for most illnesses, even minor illnesses such as colds. Most Korean hospitals will give a saline IV to patients as a complementary treatment for most illnesses.

BREAK TIME

119 [il-lil-gu]

119 is the emergency number in Korea that is used to report fires, accidents, crimes, and other emergencies. Use this number if you need an ambulance or a fire engine. 119 also serves as a number to call for hospital information. 119 provides hospital locations, specializations, and opening hours among other basic information for large-scale corporate hospitals, university hospitals, and even smaller local clinics. 119 also has English translators in addition to several other languages.

Medical Tourism

Korea is a popular medical tourism destination in Asia because of skilled doctors, modern technology, patient care services, and relatively inexpensive pricing. There are now many tourism companies that cater to medical tourists, helping to book flights, provide accommodations and transport, and find qualified doctors. Many companies also provide interpretation services.

International Clinics

While smaller hospitals may not have staff that can adequately support foreign residents and visitors, large scale hospitals have international clinics with staff who speak other languages and have been trained to converse with non-Korean patients. These international clinics cater to foreign residents and visitors of Korea and are sometimes further divided by language and country.

PHARMACY

(number of days) + - 치 [(number of days) + - chi] : (number of) days' worth of medicine

Medicine in Korea is often distributed in packets that are meant for daily consumption, making it easy for patients to remember exactly how much to take. For example, 1 packet per day or 1 packet at each meal.

Sample Sentences

이틀 **치** [i-teul chi] = two days' worth of medicine

삼일 **치** [sa-mil chi] = three days' worth of medicine

사일 **치** [sa-il chi] = four days' worth of medicine

일주일 **치** [il-ju-il chi] = one week's worth of medicine

약을 먹다 [ya-geul meok-tta] : to take medicine
약을 드시다 [ya-geul deu-si-da] : to take medicine (respectful)

The word **먹다** [meok-tta] in this phrase means literally "to eat". The respectful way to

say "to eat" is **드시다** [deu-si-da]. This Korean phrase often uses both forms of verbs, depending on the relationship between the speakers.

식후 [si-ku] : post meal

식후 is common in medication instructions from a pharmacist.

Sample Sentences

식후 30분 후에 드세요. [si-ku sam-sip-ppun hu-e deu-se-yo.] = Please take the medicine 30 minutes after you have eaten.

식후 1시간 후에 드세요. [si-ku han-si-gan hu-e deu-se-yo.] = Please take the medicine one hour after you have eaten.

Here are some common medicines that can be obtained from pharmacies without prescriptions:

감기약 [gam-gi-yak]   cold medicine

해열제 [hae-yeol-jje]	fever reducer
진통제 [jin-tong-je]	painkiller (analgesic)

Also, some medicines come in multiple forms and can be requested at pharmacies:

알약 [al-lyak]	pill, tablet
가루약 [ga-ru-yak]	powdered medicine
물약 [mul-lyak]	liquid medication
연고 [yeon-go]	ointment

약사 [yak-ssa] : pharmacist

Although most people are addressed by job title in Korea, this is not the case for pharmacists. Instead of referring the to their job title, **약사** [yak-ssa], the more general **저기요** [jeo-gi-yo], which means "excuse me", is usually used because the pharmacist is usually already there at the counter.

성분 [seong-bun] : ingredient, component

As of recently, the ingredients of medication are printed on the package. Look for the word **성분** [seong-bun] to see the components of the medicine.

밴드 [baen-deu] : adhesive bandage

BREAK TIME

Prescription
Medicine

Before July 2000, people in Korea could get medicine for most things directly from pharmacies without having to see a doctor. With the introduction of a new system in July 2000, a prescription directly from a doctor became a requirement for generic (non-branded), prescribed, and customized medication.

Nearly all Western medicine can be found in Korea but is often found under the generic name. If you need a specific brand name prescription, you will have to ask the doctor or pharmacist using the brand name so he/she can look up the generic name. Medication in Korea is usually not labeled with dosage or usage instructions, but rather placed into packets for intended for daily consumption, making written instructions unnecessary.

CAREER

SCHOOL, HAGWON, & BUSINESS

COMMON PHRASES

안녕하세요. [an-nyeong-ha-se-yo.] : Hello.

저는 (name) + -입니다. [jeo-neun (name) + -im-ni-da.] : I'm (name).

Sample Sentences

저는 Keith입니다. [jeo-neun ki-sseu-im-ni-da.] = I'm Keith.

저는 Stephanie입니다. [jeo-neun seu-te-pa-ni-im-ni-da.] = I'm Stephanie.

저는 Ben입니다. [jeo-neun be-nim-ni-da.] = I'm Ben.

이번에 새로 온 (position) + -입니다. [i-beo-ne sae-ro on (position) + -im-ni-da.] : I'm a new (position).

This phrase could be useful when introducing yourself to new co-workers. Some larger companies may ask you to introduce yourself in a group setting, but for smaller companies that don't ask for group introductions, this phrase can be used when meeting co-workers individually. Literally, **이번에** means "this time" and **새로 온** means "a new (position) that came".

Sample Sentences

이번에 새로 온 원어민 선생님입니다. [i-beo-ne sae-ro on wo-neo-min seon-saeng-ni-mim-ni-da.] = I'm a new native English teacher.

이번에 새로 온 디자이너입니다. [i-beo-ne sae-ro on di-ja-i-neo-im-ni-da.] = I'm a new designer.

이번에 새로 온 프로그래머입니다. [i-beo-ne sae-ro on peu-ro-geu-rae-meo-im-ni-da.] = I'm a new programmer.

잘 부탁 드립니다. [jal bu-tak deu-rim-ni-da.] : "Please be kind."

This phrase literally translates to "I ask a favor of you". In this instance, the favor that is being asked is to be accepted kindly into the workplace. Since this phrase is extremely broad, it can be used in a variety of workplace situations, such as at the end of a job interview or when asking someone to do some work for you.

한국어 조금 해요. [han-gu-geo jo-geum hae-yo.] : I can speak a little Korean.

한국어 잘 못해요. [han-gu-geo jal mo-tae-yo.] : I can't speak Korean well.

한국어 못 해요. [han-gu-geo mo tae-yo.] : I can't speak Korean.

(place/item) + - 어디 있어요? [(place/item) + - eo-di i-sseo-yo?] : Where is (place/item)?

Use this phrase when looking for something.

Sample Sentences

화장실 어디 있어요? [hwa-jang-sil eo-di i-sseo-yo?] = Where is the toilet?
분필 어디 있어요? [bun-pil eo-di i-sseo-yo?] = Where can I find some chalk?
그 서류 어디 있어요? [geu seo-ryu eo-di i-sseo-yo?] = Where is that document?

몸이 안 좋아서 그러는데 조퇴해도 괜찮나요? [mo-mi an jo-a-seo geu-reo-neun-de jo-toe-hae-do gwaen-chan-na-yo?] : I'm not feeling well. May I go home early today?

조퇴 means "to leave school/work early". When you have a family emergency or when you don't feel well, you can ask your boss if you can leave early by saying "조퇴해도 괜찮나요?"

Common Phrases

(date) + -에 회식이에요. [(date) + -e hoe-si-gi-e-yo.] : We are having a school/hagwon/company dinner (date).

회식 are company dinners and are an essential component of work life in Korea. The majority of Korean companies will hold company dinners at least once a month. These dinners are an important part of Korean working culture and, to some people, are even considered part of the job.

Sample Sentences

이번 금요일에 회식이에요. [i-beon geu-myo-i-re hoe-si-gi-e-yo.] = We are having a school/hagwon/company dinner this Friday.

이번 달 31일에 회식이에요. [i-beon dal sam-si-bi-ri-re hoe-si-gi-e-yo.] = We are having a school/hagwon/company dinner on the 31st of this month.

내일 회식이에요. [nae-il hoe-si-gi-e-yo.] = We are having a school/hagwon/company dinner tomorrow.

출근/퇴근 시간은 몇 시예요? [chul-geun/toe-geun si-ga-neun myeot ssi-ye-yo?] : What time should we be at work?/What time do we get off of work?

출근 and 퇴근 are words used often in the workplace. 출근 means "going to work" and 퇴근 means "getting off of work". By themselves, these terms are considered nouns, but to use as verbs, simply add 하다 [ha-da] to the end. The result is 출근하다 [chul-geun-ha-da] (to arrive at work) and 퇴근하다 [toe-geun-ha-da] (to leave work). The words 출근 and 퇴근 are often combined to become 출퇴근 [chul-toe-geun] and can be used at the beginning of this phrase to ask what time a person begins work and what time he/she gets off in the same sentence.

수고하셨습니다. [su-go-ha-syeo-sseum-ni-da.] : Good job.

This is another phrase that is used quite often in the workplace. When leaving work, many people say this phrase as a way of saying "good job on today's work" and as a way of saying "goodbye". It can also be said when any project, report, or meeting is completed.

월급 [wol-geup] : monthly paycheck

휴가 [hyu-ga] : vacation

점심 시간 [jeon-sim ssi-gan] : lunch break

야근 [ya-geun] : night overtime; working after hours

In many Korean companies, working at night after the official workday is over is not so uncommon. You will, most likely, be paid for your overtime work.

월급 [wol-geup] : monthly paycheck

휴가 [hyu-ga] : vacation

점심 시간 [jeon-sim ssi-gan] : lunch break

야근 [ya-geun] : night overtime; working after hours

BREAK TIME

The Importance of Company Dinners in Korean Culture

Company dinners are so important in the Korean working culture that some consider it to be part of the job. Most company dinners will include several "rounds" at various eating and drinking establishments (dinner at a restaurant, beer at a fried chicken bar, more drinks at karaoke, etc.), but not all company dinners are done in the same fashion. The type of dinner will depend on the type of company and the type of boss. For many larger companies, dinners will be more traditional and usually include a lot of drinking. For newer and smaller companies, a company dinner may be a night out at the movies. For the most part, company dinners are seen as a way to bond with co-workers and to build relationships. Choosing not to attend these dinners is not against company rules, but it does not look good and may give off the wrong impression. Most workers will attend company dinners and try to make the best of the situation, at least for the first "round" of dinner.

Vacation

For most companies, vacations can be used freely depending on the season and amount of work that needs to be done. This is also true for 학원 [ha-gwon] as they are not school institutions, but are actually private businesses. Public school teachers rarely use vacation days during the middle of the school year because the school's vacation days are typically in the summer and winter. If you are a public school teacher in Korea, there must be a very important and legitimate reason to use vacation days during the school year.

Working as a Foreigner in Korea

Foreigners are sometimes treated differently from Korean workers. Non-Korean people coming to work in Korea is a relatively new phenomena, and foreigners are sometimes awarded a "free pass" for cultural differences. For example, many Korean workers regard company dinners as part of their job, and it doesn't look good if they miss a dinner. For a foreigner that misses a company dinner, however, the boss may just chalk it up to a cultural misunderstanding. It's a double standard that can be both a blessing and curse.

SCHOOL & HAGWON

COMMON PHRASES

(name) + - 선생님. [(name) + - seon-saeng-nim.] : Teacher (name).

In school or academic environments, teachers are referred to by their job title, 선생님 (teacher). As with most work environments in Korea, a person's job title is typically how someone is addressed or referred to. Adding a person's name in front of the title is optional, as simply calling someone 선생님 is sufficient. Also, for certain work environments, 선생님 can be shorted to 쌤 [ssaem]. This is usually used in more casual and intimate relationships.

몸이 아파서 오늘은 학교에/학원에 못 갈 것 같아요. [mo-mi a-pa-seo o-neu-reun hak-kkyo-e/ha-gwo-ne mot gal ggeot ga-ta-yo.] : I'm not feeling well, so I don't think I can come to work today.

When it comes to taking sick days, some teaching situations are more flexible than others. At some institutions, it may be difficult to call in sick as substitute teachers may not be available.

방학은 언제부터예요? [bang-ha-geun eon-je-bu-teo-ye-yo?] : When does the vacation start?

Vacations in both public schools and private academies, 학원 [ha-gwon], are dependent on official school vacation days. During the summer and winter, public schools will be closed. During that same time, private academies may open more classes, so there may be more to do during those months.

교장 선생님 [gyo-jang seon-saeng-nim] : principal

교감 선생님 [gyo-gam seon-saeng-nim] : vice-principal

원장님 [won-jang-nim] : principal/director of a private academy (ha-gwon)
원어민 선생님 [wo-neo-min seon-saeng-nim] : native teacher

The second term refers to teachers who are native speakers of English. For many English classes in schools & academies, there is usually a two teacher system: one native English teacher to help with pronunciation and conversation, and one Korean teacher to help with grammar.

The following phrases may be useful for classroom use. However, teachers are sometimes asked not to speak Korean in the classroom. If students hear Korean from the native-English teacher, they often spend the rest of the class speaking Korean rather than using English.

숙제 했어요? [suk-jje hae-sseo-yo?] : Did you do your homework?

The first word, 숙제, means "homework", and 했어요? on it's own simply means "did you do it?" You can use this phrase in a more general way by removing 숙제 from the phrase and applying toward any in-class assignments or projects.

(number) + – 쪽 펴세요. [(number) + – jjok pyeo-se-yo.] : **Please open to page (number).**

질문 있어요? [jil-mu ni-sseo-yo?] : **Do you have any questions?**

이해됐어요? [i-hae-dwae-sseo-yo?] : **Do you understand?**

조용히 하세요. [jo-yong-hi ha-se-yo.] : **Please be quiet.**

정답 아는 사람? [jeong-dap a-neun sa-ram?] : **Who knows the answer?**

정답 means "correct answer". If you've asked a question and a student gets the correct answer, you can say the word 정답 on its own to tell a student that the answer is correct.

잘 모르겠어요. [jal mo-reu-ge-sseo-yo.] : **I don't understand.**

This phrase may be said by students. You may also hear a more direct way of saying "I don't understand" or "I don't know", 몰라요 [mol-la-yo].

(number) + -학년 (number) + -반 [(number) + -hang-nyeon (number) + -ban)] : class (number) in (number)th grade

School classes in Korea are numbered using this system. The school grade and year are stated, followed by the class number.

More Words

수업 [su-eop]	class
쉬는 시간 [swi-neun si-gan]	recess
학생 [hak-ssaeng]	student
교실 [gyo-sil]	classroom
교무실 [gyo-mu-sil]	teacher's room
영어 [yeong-eo]	the English language
교과서 [gyo-gwa-seo]	textbook
칠판 [chil-pan]	blackboard
분필 [bun-pil]	chalk
물백묵 [mul-baeng-muk]	liquid chalk marker

BREAK TIME

Hagwon (학원)

Hagwon (**학원**) is a large part of Korea's shadow education system. In addition to regular schooling, the vast majority of Korean students attend privately owned after school academies, called **학원**, for all types of subjects (math, English, science, history, etc.) Most students are enrolled in several academies at once in hopes of gaining an advantage over other students. However, since most students attend academies, it is considered as just keeping up with the rest of the students.

Visas for Teaching in Korea

The E-2 visa is the most common visa for English teachers in Korea. Korean law dictates that these visas can only be issued to citizens of the following countries: Australia, Canada, New Zealand, South Africa, United Kingdom, United States, and Ireland. A teacher must also have a bachelor's degree and a diploma with an apostille. Additionally, there must be a certified criminal background check from your home country as well as a medical check upon arrival in Korea.

Another option is the E-1 visa. Although it is intended for people with a PhD, those with master's degrees (usually in related subjects) are also eligible for the E-1 visa. This visa is meant for university teachers and professors and requires no criminal background or medical checks.

BUSINESS

IN THE OFFICE

In many Korean companies, and especially large ones, official titles are very important and employees are expected to remember the title of a co-worker along with their name. Sometimes titles are attached after the full name of a certain person, for example 김 주영+과장님 [gim-ju-yeong] (name)+[gwa-jang-nim] (title). Often times, however, a person's given name is dropped and the surname (last name) is followed by the title, such as in 김 과장님 [gim gwa-jang-nim] (in Korea, the surname comes first and the given name after).

Although the titles can differ depending on the company, the following are the most common office titles that are used in Korean workplaces. Titles can be used without the word –님 [nim] except when you are addressing someone who is above you in the office hierarchy. Using –님 is a formality and a sign of respect.

대리님 [dae-rin-nim]

대리 [dae-ri] is someone who is not a rookie (신입 사원 [si-nip sa-won]) and has two or more years of experience on the job but has not yet been promoted to section chief. The original meaning is "deputy section chief", but many companies have multiple 대리 in one section, thus making 대리 a very broad term used to refer to someone who is not in a managing position.

팀장님 [tim-jang-nim]

팀 [tim] comes from the English word "team" and 팀장 is the "head" of a team. Depending on the structure of the company, a 팀 can be either smaller or larger than a 과 [gwa] (section). There are certain smaller companies or organizations where every single member is addressed as a 팀장. In this case, using the term 팀장 sounds more professional than just using a person's name.

과장님 [gwa-jang-nim]

In a relatively large Korean company, most employees will either be a **신입 사원** [si-nip sa-won] (rookie) or **대리**. When a **대리** stays at the company for long enough and gets promoted, s/he becomes a **과장** (section chief).

차장님 [cha-jang-nim]

차장 is the deputy head of a department, assuming that a "department" (**부**) is larger than a "section" (**과**) in a particular company.

부장님 [bu-jang-nim]

부장 is the head of a department.

이사님 [i-san-nim], 상무님 [sang-mun-nim], 대표님 [dae-pyon-nim]

이사 is a title for directors or board members. There can be many different types of **이사**, including **상무 이사** [sang-mu i-sa] (executive director) and **대표 이사** [dae-pyo i-sa] (chief executive officer, or CEO). These term are commonly shortened to **상무** and **대표** respectively.

사장님 [sa-jang-nim]

The owner of a large corporation is always addressed as **대표님** or **대표 이사님** [dae-pyo i-san-nim], but the owner of a private company or a store is called **사장님**.

Take a look at some of the phrases you might need to use while working in an office setting.

알려 주세요. [al-lyeo ju-se-yo.] : Please teach me.

What you are asking to be taught does not have to be explicitly mentioned and can be understood from the context. For example, if you are asked to write a report, this phrase can be understood as "Please teach me (how to write the report)".

이거 어떻게 해요? [i-geo eo-tteo-ke hae-yo?] : How do we do this?

This phrase can be used both at work and outside of work. In the workplace, this phrase is useful for asking how to do things the correct way (using a photocopy machine, printing, etc.) Outside of work, you can use this phrase when you want to learn to use something, such as a rice cooker or ATM machine.

누구 담당이에요? [nu-gu dam-dang-i-e-yo?] / 담당자가 누구예요?
[dam-dang-ja-ga nu-gu-ye-yo?] : Who's in charge of this?

Use this phrase to ask for the person in charge of a certain project or work. A person who is in charge is called a 담당자 [dam-dang-ja]. This phrase is useful when collaborating with other departments or working with other companies.

결재해 주세요. [gyeol-jjae-hae ju-se-yo.] : Please authorize/
approve.

In many work situations, there will be times when authorization or approval is necessary. This phrase can be used to get approval for documents or certain orders from managers or bosses.

(date) (time) + -에 회의 있어요. [(date) (time) + -e hoe-ui i-sseo-yo.]
: We have a meeting (or) (date) at (time).

Sample Sentences

내일 3시에 회의 있어요. [nae-il se-si-e hoe-ui i-sseo-yo.] = We have a meeting tomorrow at three.

이번 금요일 4시에 회의 있어요. [i-beon geu-myo-il ne-si-e hoe-ui i-sseo-yo.] = We have a meeting this Friday at four.

오늘 6시에 회의 있어요. [o-neul yeo-seo-ssi-e hoe-ui i-sseo-yo.] = We have a meeting six o'clock today.

이메일로 보내 주세요. [i-me-il-lo bo-nae ju-se-yo.] : Please send it via e-mail.

문자 [mun-jja] (text messages) and 팩스 [paek-sseu] (fax) are alternatives to e-mail.

문자로 보내 주세요. [mun-jja-ro bo-nae-ju-se-yo]: Please send it via text message.

팩스로 보내 주세요. [paek-sseu-ro bo-nae ju-se-yo]: Please send it via fax.

복사 좀 해 주세요. [bok-ssa jom hae ju-se-yo.] : Please copy this.

This phrase is used when asking someone to make copies for you. You can be more specific with the amount the copies you need by saying the number of copies you need: (1) 한 장 [han jang], (2) 두 장 [du jang], (3) 세 장 [se jang], (4) 네 장 [ne jang], (5) 다섯 장 [da-seot jjang], etc.

Office Supplies

호치키스 [ho-chi-ki-seu]	stapler
스카치테이프 [seu-ka-chi-te-i-peu]	tape
볼펜 [bol-pen]	pen
파일 [pa-il]	folder

서류 [seo-ryu]	document
계약서 [gye-yak-sseo]	contract
컴퓨터 [keom-pyu-teo]	computer
서랍 [seo-rap]	drawer
책상 [chaek-ssang] / **데스크** [de-seu-keu]	desk
의자 [eui-ja]	chair
자리 [ja-ri]	seat
프린터 [peu-rin-teo]	printer
복사기 [bok-ssa-gi]	copy machine
냉장고 [naeng-jang-go]	refrigerator
A4 용지 [e-i-po yong-ji]	A4 size paper

Other Useful Words

사무실 [sa-mu-sil]	office
점심 [jeom-sim]	lunch

BUSINESS TRIP

세미나에 참석하러 왔어요. [se-mi-na-e cham-seo-ka-reo wa-sseo-yo.] : I'm here to attend a seminar.

"…참석하러 왔어요" means "I'm here to attend …". You can replace the word 세미나 with 회의 [hoe-ui] (meeting), 컨벤션 [keon-ben-syeon] (convention), or other events related to your visit.

저는 (name of your company) + -에서 온 (name) + -입니다. [jeo-neun (name of your company) + -e-seo on (name) + -im-ni-da] : I'm (name) from (name of your company).

This is a simple, straightforward, and polite way to introduce yourself. It makes your work affiliation clear while introducing your name at the same time.

명함 [myeong-ham] : business card

Business cards are a vital part of doing any type of business in Korea. If you are coming to Korea on business, remember to have plenty of business cards on hand.

Sample Sentences

제 명함입니다. [je myeong-ham-im-ni-da] = This is my business card.

제가 명함 드렸나요? [je-ga myeong-ham deu-ryeon-na-yo?] = Have I already given you my business card?

명함 하나 주실 수 있나요? [myeong-ham ha-na ju-sil ssu in-na-yo?] = Can I have your business card?

BREAK TIME

Snack Sharing

If someone buys snacks during working hours, it is common courtesy in Korean culture to buy more for other workers. For larger companies, just buying for your team or people in your immediate vicinity should be enough. For smaller companies, buying for all the workers may be a good idea. Nearly all workers in a Korean office will, at some time or another, receive snacks and drinks from other workers. While buying snacks for other workers is not considered a rule, returning the favor is looked favorably upon.

Business Cards

There is a general ritual for giving and receiving business cards in Korea. When meeting someone for the first time for business purposes, business cards are expected to be exchanged. Business cards are received and given with two hands. When the cards are received, it's common for people to analyze the card and to mentally take note of the person's position and status. Finally, after a thoughtful look, when it is time to put away the business card, do so discreetly. Business cards are sometimes considered to be an extension of a person, and as such, should be respected.

Titles

Typically, entry level workers at most companies will often refer to each other by name and add 씨 [ssi] to the end to show respect. For example, 정은 씨 [jeong-eun ssi], David 씨 [de-i-bi-deu ssi], etc. However, for higher level workers (managers, vice presidents, etc.), titles are used instead of given names. Calling a higher level worker by his/her name can be seen as disrespectful.

SURVIVAL KOREAN

for Travelers and Expats
Phrases and tips to make your stay in Korea easy

| 1판 1쇄 | 1st edition published | 2014. 6. 16. |
| 1판 11쇄 | 11th edition published | 2023. 10. 2. |

지은이	Written by	TalkToMeInKorean, Keith Kim
책임편집	Edited by	안효진 Hyojin An, 스테파니 베이츠 Stephanie Bates
디자인	Designed by	김민재 Minjae Kim
표지 그림	Cover Illustrations by	장성원 Sungwon Jang
사진 편집	Photographs Edited by	나니야 NANIYA
펴낸곳	Published by	롱테일북스 Longtail Books
펴낸이	Publisher	이수영 Su Young Lee
편집	Copy-edited by	김보경 Florence Kim
주소	Address	04033 서울특별시 마포구 양화로 113, 3층(서교동, 순흥빌딩)
		3rd Floor, 113 Yanghwa-ro, Mapo-gu, Seoul, KOREA
이메일	E-mail	TTMIK@longtailbooks.co.kr
ISBN		978-89-5605-736-1 13710

*이 교재의 내용을 사전 허가 없이 전재하거나 복제할 경우 법적인 제재를 받게 됨을 알려 드립니다.

*잘못된 책은 구입하신 서점이나 본사에서 교환해 드립니다.

*정가는 표지에 표시되어 있습니다.